Year **3**

The Church Begins

STUDENT GUIDE

> Forever, O LORD, Your word is settled in heaven.
> Your faithfulness endures to all generations; You
> established the earth, and it abides.—Psalm 119:89–90

GOD'S WORD FOR ALL GENERATIONS

Answers
BIBLE CURRICULUM

Answers Bible Curriculum

Year 3 • Quarter 3 • Adult Student

For more information write:
Answers in Genesis
PO Box 510
Hebron, KY 41048

Printed in China.

Contents

Introduction to Answers Bible Curriculum. 5

1   Final Passover and Betrayal 7

    Prepare to Learn 8
    Studying God's Word. 11
    Our Passover Lamb. 11
    God's Word in the Real World 13
    Prayer Requests 14

2   God's Plan Unfolds 15

    Prepare to Learn 16
    Studying God's Word. 19
    The Trials of Jesus 19
    God's Word in the Real World 20
    Prayer Requests 20

3   Peter's Denial. 23

    Prepare to Learn 24
    Studying God's Word. 27
    God's Restoring Grace. 27
    God's Word in the Real World 27
    Prayer Requests 28

4   The Crucifixion 29

    Prepare to Learn 30
    Studying God's Word. 33
    A Prophetic Death 34
    God's Word in the Real World 34
    Prayer Requests 36

5   The Resurrection 37

    Prepare to Learn 38
    Studying God's Word. 41
    A Risen Savior. 41
    God's Word in the Real World 43
    Prayer Requests 44

6   The Great Commission. 45

    Prepare to Learn 46
    Studying God's Word. 49
    Whose Commission?. 49
    God's Word in the Real World 51
    Prayer Requests 52

7   **Resurrection Theories** 53
     Prepare to Learn 54
     Studying God's Word. 57
     Resurrection Theories Video. 57
     God's Word in the Real World 58
     Prayer Requests 58

8   **The Promised Helper Comes** 59
     Prepare to Learn 60
     Studying God's Word. 63
     The Work of the Spirit. 63
     God's Word in the Real World 65
     Prayer Requests 66

9   **The Apostles Are Persecuted.** 67
     Prepare to Learn 68
     Studying God's Word. 71
     Facing Persecution 71
     God's Word in the Real World 73
     Prayer Requests 74

10   **The Gospel Spreads.** 75
     Prepare to Learn 76
     Studying God's Word. 79
     Providential Outcomes. 80
     God's Word in the Real World 81
     Prayer Requests 82

11   **Saul Is Converted** 83
     Prepare to Learn 84
     Studying God's Word. 87
     Testimony of Mercy 88
     God's Word in the Real World 89
     Prayer Requests 90

12   **The Gospel Goes to the Gentiles** 91
     Prepare to Learn 92
     Studying God's Word. 95
     Pick and Choose 95
     God's Word in the Real World 95
     Prayer Requests 96

Introduction to Answers Bible Curriculum

Jesus's earthly ministry was coming to an end. He had lived a perfect life. His amazing miracles had demonstrated His power and deity. His startling teachings had amazed the people . . . and enraged the religious leaders. Jesus would give His life willingly as He was sentenced to death by crucifixion. His death on the Cross secured eternal redemption for all sinners who would turn to Him in repentance and faith. And his Resurrection from the dead secured the promise of eternal life and gives all believers living hope.

After His sacrificial death and Resurrection from the dead, Jesus ascended to the Father, but not before leaving His followers with a command: "Go therefore and make disciples of all the nations, baptizing them in the name of the Father and of the Son and of the Holy Spirit, teaching them to observe all things that I have commanded you; and lo, I am with you always, even to the end of the age" (Matthew 28:19–20). Because of the power of God's indwelling Holy Spririt, the early church spread the good news of the gospel far and wide. Even in the midst of persecution, God used these faithful men and women to expand His church.

We encourage you to read the Prepare to Learn section before class each week. This will provide important background information so that you will get more from each lesson.

For more information and links to online articles and videos, be sure to visit the Online Resource Page at www.AnswersBibleCurriculum.com.

Final Passover and Betrayal

1

Key Passages

- Matthew 26:14–30; John 18:1–11; 1 Corinthians 11:23–26

What You Will Learn

- How the final Passover—the Lord's Supper—is a remembrance of Jesus's death.

- How Judas's betrayal was part of God's plan.

Lesson Overview

During His last Passover meal, and just before He was betrayed in the garden, Jesus shared bread and wine with His apostles. The blessing and eating together of this meal pointed to the suffering He was about to endure on the Cross. Jesus commanded them to continue to use bread and wine to remember His sacrifice. Today, we do that with communion, also called the Lord's Supper. That same evening Jesus was betrayed in the garden by Judas who led the troops to arrest Him. Jesus willingly submitted, knowing it was the Father's plan.

Memory Verse

Matthew 28:18–20

And Jesus came and spoke to them, saying, "All authority has been given to Me in heaven and on earth. Go therefore and make disciples of all the nations, baptizing them in the name of the Father and of the Son and of the Holy Spirit, teaching them to observe all things that I have commanded you; and lo, I am with you always, even to the end of the age." Amen.

 Prepare to Learn

SCRIPTURAL BACKGROUND

Jesus knew why He had come. He was committed to perfect obedience to His Father's will, which included His death on the Cross followed by His Resurrection from the grave. He knew the time had come, and His face was steadfastly set to go to Jerusalem—the place where His life of obedience would dramatically end (Luke 9:51). It was here in Jerusalem where Jesus celebrated the Passover meal—the last meal He would share with His closest friends.

The Jewish Passover was the most honored and sacred times of sacrifice. It was a holiday celebrated by the Jews to remember God's deliverance of the Israelites from slavery out of Egypt. Detailed instructions for this holiday were passed down from the Lord and began at that first Passover. The first Passover recorded preceded the last of God's plagues on Egypt—when the firstborn of every household would be struck down. The sacrificial instructions from God for that first Passover were specific, including which animal to sacrifice, what to do with its blood, how to cook it, what to do with the leftovers, what to wear, why to prepare in haste, and what the shed blood represented (Exodus 12).

God demanded that the Passover sacrifice be an unblemished lamb (Exodus 12:5). The blood of that lamb would be put on the doorframe of the Israelites' homes. That blood would be a sign, and the destroyer would pass over those homes and spare those within (Exodus 12:13). And this was what the Passover holiday would remind the Jews of each year.

The lesson of the Passover was that God's wrath could only be satisfied by the death and shedding of innocent blood—in this case the blood of a lamb. Although this sacrifice was repeated year after year, the blood of the lamb would not ultimately satisfy God's wrath. The Bible tells us these sacrifices were a foreshadowing of the good things to come. They could never perfectly cover the sins of the people—or why would they be made year after year? The Bible tells us that it is impossible for the blood of animals to take away sins (Hebrews 10:1–4). No, these sacrifices pointed to another—the Lord Jesus Christ—who was put to death once for all, that He might bring sinners to God (1 Peter 3:18).

This is the gospel! In this upper room with His disciples, at this last Passover dinner—the Last Supper—Jesus was preparing Himself and His followers for His death. The annual sacrifices of the traditional Passover celebration would no longer be necessary. For the perfect Lamb of God would soon be slain and bring salvation to those whose names are written in the Lamb's Book of Life (Revelation 3:5, 13:8).

As we consider this memorable meal, we can't help but think of the betrayal that would soon complete God's remarkable plan of redemption—a plan to kill His only Son (John 18:11). God the Father used Judas the betrayer to hand over the Redeemer of the world to death so that sinners could be reconciled back to God and forgiven for all of eternity. This is the plan that God Himself had predestined from before the creation of the world (Acts 2:22–23; Ephesians 1:4–5).

Today, Christians gather around the table of the Lord to remember Jesus's final sacrifice. We eat the bread, and we drink the cup as we proclaim the Lord's death (1 Corinthians 11:26), waiting expectantly for His victorious return (Matthew 24:27; 1 Thessalonians 4:16–17).

HISTORICAL/APOLOGETICS BACKGROUND

The Lord's Supper (also called Communion and the Eucharist) is usually considered one of the two sacraments or ordinances that Jesus gave to His church (the other being baptism). Churches across the world celebrate the Lord's Supper, some quarterly, some monthly, some weekly, and some at every meal.

During Jesus's final Passover meal with His disciples, He instituted the Lord's Supper. And as they were eating, Jesus took bread, blessed and broke it, and gave it to the disciples and said, "Take, eat; this is My body." Then He took the cup, and gave thanks, and gave it to them, saying, "Drink from it, all of you. For this is My blood of the new covenant, which is shed for many for the remission of sins" (Matthew 26:26–28).

There are four basic views among Christians on the meaning of our Lord's words. The Roman Catholic Church teaches a view called transubstantiation where the substance, or the essence, of the bread and wine are transformed into the physical body and blood of Christ. In Rome's view the bread and wine actually become the body and blood of Christ, but the appearance to our senses remains like bread and wine. It is also believed that through the Eucharist, the benefits of Christ's death on the cross are being given over and over for the payment of each person's sins. In other words, Christ is being sacrificed anew each time Communion is served.

Most Protestants reject transubstantiation for several reasons. First of all, we must understand that Christ cannot be, nor should He ever be, offered up over and over for the payment of sins.

Scripture is very clear that Jesus's sacrifice on the Cross was a one-time offering for sin that never needs to be repeated (Hebrews 7:25–27, 9:28, 10:10–14). Secondly, this belief of transubstantiation attests to the idea that Jesus's body and blood are present on the altar each time someone celebrates the Lord's Supper. We know, in fact, that Jesus is with us on earth through His indwelling Holy Spirit. But Jesus, the Son, in His humanity, is not on earth but in heaven at the right hand of God the Father (Ephesians 1:20; Colossians 3:1). And He will not return to earth until His glorious Second Coming (Hebrews 9:28; Titus 2:13).

The other positions mentioned below are considered orthodox views. Martin Luther taught the idea of consubstantiation. Those holding to this position believe that the fundamental "substance" of the body and blood of Christ are present alongside the substance of the bread and wine, which remain present. In this view, the substance of Christ's body and blood exist "in, with, and under" the substance of regular bread and wine. So Communion becomes fully bread and wine, and fully Christ, just as Christ Himself is fully human and fully God at the same time. Thus, the body and blood of Christ are truly received in the Lord's Supper making it a means of grace for the Christian's sanctification. But the bread and wine don't literally become the body and blood of Jesus.

Most evangelicals hold to a view promoted by Swiss Reformer Ulrich Zwingli, which is called the Symbolic or Memorial view. This view denies the bodily presence of the Lord in the Lord's Supper and instead interprets Jesus's words in a figurative sense. In this view, the Lord's Supper is seen primarily as a commemoration or a heightened remembering of His sacrifice, but there is no presence of Christ in the elements.

The Lord's Supper is seen not as a direct experience with the body and blood of Christ but as a memorial service.

Another important and widely held view of the Lord's Supper is the view articulated by French theologian, John Calvin. This view has been called the Real Presence, which is somewhat of an intermediate view between Luther on one side and the Memorial view on the other. Calvin rejected the idea that there is a transformation of substance of the elements, but he also rejected the view that the Lord's Supper is merely a remembrance of a past event using symbols and figurative language. Calvin insisted on the real, though spiritual, presence of the Lord in the elements. He understood the Lord's Supper to be an actual means of grace through which the Lord imparts His sanctifying grace to the believer who faithfully partakes of it.

Ultimately, the Lord's Supper looks backward to what Jesus accomplished on the Cross, where His body was broken, and His blood was shed to provide eternal redemption. But it also looks forward in anticipation of the future messianic banquet. This expectation is expressed in the Gospels by Christ's words: "Assuredly, I say to you, I will no longer drink of the fruit of the vine until that day when I drink it new in the kingdom of God" (Mark 14:25). In his letter to the Corinthians, Paul expressed this expectation with the phrase, "For as often as you eat this bread and drink this cup, you proclaim the Lord's death till He comes" (1 Corinthians 11:26).

The Lord's Supper is also to be a time of self-examination. Paul told these Corinthian believers, "But let a man examine himself, and so let him eat of the bread and drink of the cup" (1 Corinthians 11:28). We are not to take Communion lightly, but it should be a time of self-examination, confession of sin, and repentance as we remember Christ's sacrifice on our behalf.

As Christians we solemnly and joyfully partake of the Lord's Supper because it represents the redemption that Christ has already provided. And it represents the eternal hope we have in the joyful journey leading to a happy reunion with the Savior at the celebration of the marriage supper of the Lamb (Revelation 19:9).

See the Online Resource Page for more information on this topic.

 Studying God's Word

Should we be observing the Passover today?

_____

Take notes as you study the following passages.

Matthew 26:14–30

_____

_____

Exodus 12

_____

_____

1 Corinthians 11:23–26

_____

_____

 Our Passover Lamb

Throughout the New Testament there are many connections made between the Passover and Jesus. For the following topics, identify the ideas from Scripture that relate Jesus to the Passover. Where you can, note any specific passages that express each idea. (Don't be afraid to use the concordance or topical index in the back of your Bible or cross-references in Exodus 12.)

Begin by reading through Exodus 12:1–20. As you read, be on the lookout for ideas that are parallel to the character of Jesus and the work He accomplished on our behalf.

1. Character of the lamb (12:5)

2. Application of the blood (12:7)

3. Effect of the blood (12:13)

4. Memorial feast (12:14–17)

Can you think of any other parallels that would be helpful in understanding the connections between the Old Covenant and the New Covenant?

Write a summary statement that connects the Passover to Jesus.

Take notes as you study the following passages.
John 18:1-11

_____

_____

_____

Mark 14:48-49

_____

_____

_____

Acts 2:22–23

_____

_____

_____

 God's Word in the Real World

1. How does the connection between the Passover and the Lord's Supper help you to better appreciate what Jesus has done on your behalf?

2. How could you use the parallels between the Passover and the Lord's Supper to encourage a brother or sister in Christ?

3. As you consider how Jesus approached His arrest, knowing fully what was about to happen, how does this impact the way you think about living your life in service to Him?

4. As crude as it may sound, some radical skeptics accuse Christians of being cannibals or acting like zombies who eat the flesh of a dead god during Communion. This was also a misunderstanding in the early years of the church leading to a social stigma on Christians. How would you respond to someone who made such claims about you?

5. The Roman Catholic Church teaches that the Eucharist is much more than a memorial meal shared by Christians, but that the bread and wine actually become the body and blood of Christ that is being offered again as a sacrifice by the priest during each Mass. This view is called *transubstantiation* and is thought to be a necessary practice to remain in a state of grace before God. What errors do you see in this view? How would you use Scripture to help a Roman Catholic see the errors?

Prayer Requests

2
God's Plan Unfolds

Key Passages

- Matthew 26:57–68; John 18:28–19:26

What You Will Learn

- Why the Jewish leaders condemned Jesus.
- How God was in charge of all that happened to Jesus.

Lesson Overview

The events leading up to the Cross were unfolding according to God's plan. The Jewish leaders wanted Jesus dead for blasphemy—for claiming to be the Messiah, the Son of God. They tried Him and brought Him to Pilate who also questioned Him. Jesus remained obedient and trusted the Father's will.

Memory Verse

Matthew 28:18–20

And Jesus came and spoke to them, saying, "All authority has been given to Me in heaven and on earth. Go therefore and make disciples of all the nations, baptizing them in the name of the Father and of the Son and of the Holy Spirit, teaching them to observe all things that I have commanded you; and lo, I am with you always, even to the end of the age." Amen.

Prepare to Learn

SCRIPTURAL BACKGROUND

The hour had come, and the Savior celebrated His last Passover in the upper room with His closest friends and Judas the betrayer (Luke 22:14). Jesus knew He would soon be betrayed (Luke 22:21), arrested (John 18:12), and killed (John 19:16). He knew also that this was the cup which His Father had given Him to drink (John 18:11).

The Bible tells us that many people were gathered together against Jesus to destroy Him—both Herod and Pontius Pilate, with the Gentiles and the people of Israel (Acts 4:27). Ultimately, it was the Roman governor Pilate who gave the actual order to execute the Savior (John 19:16). But it was the Jewish high priest, the priests, the scribes, the Pharisees, and the Jewish people who relentlessly demanded that Jesus be killed (John 18:30, 19:15). The Jewish leaders had previously conspired with the high priest and plotted to take Jesus and kill Him (Matthew 26:3–4). These were the very people who had waited centuries for the Messiah to come and save them.

What had Jesus done that would incite the Jewish leaders to such hostility? We find the answer in Scripture, of course. Many of the Jews were furious with Jesus's claim to be God! They accused Him of blasphemy when Jesus forgave the sins of the paralytic—blasphemy because only God could forgive sins (Matthew 9:2–3). When Jesus admitted that He knew God, He was from God, and God had sent Him, the Jews sought to take Him. But it was not yet His hour (John 7:29–30).

When Jesus called Himself the great I AM, this led the Jews to take up stones to kill Him (John 8:58–59). And when Jesus made the statement, "I and My Father are one," the Jews again were provoked to stone Him (John 10:30–31). These Jews understood Jesus's claim that He was God! But they would not believe it. And this is why they demanded His death.

But there was another purpose in their hatred of Jesus—that Scripture might be fulfilled. Jesus told His disciples that one of the reasons the world hated both Him and His Father was, "that the word might be fulfilled which is written in their law, 'They hated Me without a cause'" (John 15:25). This quote of Psalm 69:4 demonstrates that even in the Jews' unfounded hatred of Jesus, God was at work fulfilling His Word.

So when His hour had finally come—according to the perfect plan of God—they were all too ready to accuse Jesus and see Him crucified. Jesus was betrayed and arrested in the garden (John 18:12). Then He was brought before the Jewish leader Annas (John 18:13), and then delivered to Caiaphas the high priest (John 18:24). From there He went to Pilate, the governor (John 18:28–29). Pilate sent Him to Herod who had jurisdiction over Galilee (Luke 23:8). Herod sent Him back to Pilate (Luke 23:11). Here Jesus was subjected to more torture, ridicule, and humiliation and was finally delivered over to be crucified (John 19:1–16).

What a horrible crime and sin against the Son of God! And yet, the Scriptures tell us that this was all accomplished perfectly and according to God's determined purpose and foreknowledge (Acts 2:23). Jesus came to do the perfect will of God in perfect obedience, even to the point of death—death on a cross (Philippians 2:8).

Jesus knew what He must do. Even in the garden during the betrayal, while

Peter wanted to defend Jesus with the sword, Jesus's response was that He must drink this cup that His Father had given to Him (John 18:11).

God was in control of all that was happening. Even this worst of all evils was under the sovereign hand of God the Father. Jesus knew this and made it clear to Pilate when He answered him and said, "You could have no power over me unless it had been given you from above" (John 19:11a).

The trial and death of Jesus Christ should always bring us to the remembrance of the gospel. For in spite of the Jews, the Gentiles, the Pharisees, the Romans, and all those directly responsible for Jesus's death, we are told in Scripture that while we were still sinners, Jesus died for us (Romans 5:8). That means it was our sins that caused His death; it was for our sins that Jesus was punished. As the writer of the song, "How Deep the Father's Love for Us," so movingly penned:

It was my sin that held Him there
Until it was accomplished.
His dying breath has brought me life;
I know that it is finished.

For He Himself bore our sins in His body on the tree that we might live (1 Peter 2:24). It is only through Jesus's death and Resurrection that sinners could ever be reconciled to God and receive the hope of eternal life.

HISTORICAL/APOLOGETICS BACKGROUND

Few people realize it, but the trial of Jesus was not a single trial, but six different trials—three before the Jewish religious authorities and three before the Roman secular authorities. All of these trials were illegal and unjust according to Jewish law and tradition.

Jesus was charged before the Jewish leaders for blasphemy, claiming to be the Son of God, the Messiah (Mark 14:60–63). The three Jewish trials included His appearance before Annas, the former high priest (John 18:12–13); Caiaphas, the current high priest, and the Sanhedrin—an assembly of religious leaders (John 18:19–24; Matthew 26:57).

After these trials, Jesus was taken before the Roman authorities where the charges brought against Him were quite different. Jesus was charged with ". . . perverting the nation, and forbidding to pay taxes to Caesar, saying that He Himself is Christ a King" (Luke 23:2). These trials took place before Pilate, the Roman governor (John 18:29), Herod (Luke 23:7), and then Pilate again (Luke 23:11–12).

The Bible reports that Pilate found no fault with Jesus (Luke 23:4). And yet the people insisted that Pilate do something. So Pilate delivered Him to Herod, who had jurisdiction over Galilee (Luke 23:7). Herod questioned Jesus. He, too was influenced by the chief priests and scribes who stood and vehemently accused Jesus (Luke 23:10). But again, Jesus was found innocent of any crime worthy of crucifixion. Herod sent Jesus back to Pilate—and Pilate said again that he could find no fault in Jesus that was deserving of death (Luke 23:14–15). In fact, the Bible states that Pilate wished to release Jesus. But the people were still shouting that He be crucified! Again, Pilate repeated that Jesus had done no evil (Luke 23:20–22). In a final effort to have Jesus released, Pilate offered the prisoner Barabbas to be crucified. But the crowds called for Barabbas to be released and Jesus to be crucified. Pilate finally granted their demand and surrendered Jesus to their will (Luke 23:25).

The trials before the Jewish authorities and the Romans were remarkably unjust and illegal. The animosity of the Jewish leaders toward Jesus is clearly evident in the process they followed as they blatantly disregarded many of their own laws. Scholars and historians have noted a number of violations of Jewish law in these trials.

Jesus was arrested illegally. He was arrested secretly, at night, on no formal charge of any crime, by those who were to be His judges. All of these points were against Jewish law.

Jesus was tried illegally. He was tried at night, in secret, and on the eve of a Sabbath during feast time—all of which violated Jewish law.

Jesus was indicted illegally. He was charged for a crime based on His own statements. The court indicted Jesus with no supporting evidence whatsoever, and the witnesses against Him were found to be false witnesses whose statements conflicted.

Jesus was convicted illegally. He was convicted by the Sanhedrin as a group. But each member of the court was supposed to vote individually to convict or acquit. It was also illegal because the merits of Jesus's defense were not considered.

Jesus was sentenced illegally. He was sentenced to death in a place forbidden by law. A sentence of death could only be pronounced in a court, but Jesus was sentenced at the home of the high priest. It was also illegal because a sentence of death could not be carried out until the following day; only a few hours passed before Jesus was placed on the Cross.

Clearly, these trials of Jesus represent the ultimate mockery of justice. Jesus, the only innocent man ever to have lived, was found guilty and sentenced to death by crucifixion.

The irony of the situation is that those who misjudged Jesus will be judged rightly by Him some day. The tables will be turned. Jesus's judges were nothing but criminals, and they will be justly condemned if they remained in their unbelief. Jesus told the Jewish leaders that God "has committed all judgment to the Son" (John 5:22). The Apostle Paul told the men of Athens that God "has appointed a day on which He will judge the world in righteousness by the Man [Jesus] whom He has ordained" (Acts 17:31). We can be assured that no matter the injustices we experience, one day all will be made right. Jesus will judge the world in righteousness, and all the scales will be balanced.

For more information on this topic, see the Online Resource Page.

Studying God's Word

How many trials did Jesus face?

_____

The Trials of Jesus

If you were to read only one of the Gospel accounts of the trials of Jesus, you would not get the full picture. Taken as a whole, the four Gospel accounts present six trials that Jesus faced between His arrest in the Garden of Gethsemane and His Crucifixion.

For each of the passages below, note who tried Jesus and describe the treatment He received.

1. John 18:1–3

2. John 18:12–13, 18:19–23

3. Matthew 26:57–68

4. Luke 22:66–71

5. Luke 23:1–7

6. Luke 23:8–12

7. Luke 23:13–25

Take notes as you study the following passages.

Matthew 26:57–68

_____

_____

_____

_____

John 18:28–19:26

_____

_____

_____

_____

 ## God's Word in the Real World

1. As you think about all that Jesus endured from His arrest and through the trials, how does it help you to appreciate what Christ has done for you?

2. Had you been in the crowd before Pilate, how do you think you would have responded to his offer to release Jesus?

3. How do the details recorded in the Bible regarding Jesus's trials confirm the authenticity and authority of the Bible?

4. The Jews had been waiting for the Messiah for thousands of years. As Jesus walked among them, He healed people, performed miracles, announced the kingdom of God, and taught them truth from the Father tightly connected to the Old Testament. As you think about the situation that the Jewish leaders were in, why do you think they missed the fact that He was the Messiah, charging Him with blasphemy and seeking to kill Him?

5. If the Jews had performed the execution according to their own law, Jesus would have died by stoning. Why would this have been an impossible outcome?

6. In the past, some historians doubted the authenticity of the account of Jesus's trials before Pilate because there was no evidence outside of the Bible that there was a governor named Pilate. In 1961, a stone was found inscribed with "Tiberieum, [Pon]tius Pilatus, [Praef]ectus Iuda[eae]" (translated; Pontius Pilate, Governor of Judea under Tiberius). Did this discovery prove that Jesus was actually tried by Pilate?

Prayer Requests

3 Peter's Denial

Key Passages

- Mark 14:26–31, 14:53–54, 14:66–72; John 21:1–19

What You Will Learn

- How Peter denied Jesus.
- How Jesus restored Peter.

Lesson Overview

The night Jesus was arrested, Peter followed behind Jesus and the guards to see what would happen. As Peter waited in the courtyard, he was recognized as one of Jesus's disciples. Peter denied knowing Jesus three times in a row that evening because he was afraid. When he realized what he had done, he wept and was sorry. Later, after the Resurrection, Jesus appeared to Peter, and Peter was able to tell his Lord that he loved him! Three times Jesus asked if Peter loved Him. Three times Peter answered yes! Jesus forgave Peter and commissioned him as a leader in the church.

Memory Verse

Matthew 28:18–20

And Jesus came and spoke to them, saying, "All authority has been given to Me in heaven and on earth. Go therefore and make disciples of all the nations, baptizing them in the name of the Father and of the Son and of the Holy Spirit, teaching them to observe all things that I have commanded you; and lo, I am with you always, even to the end of the age." Amen.

 Prepare to Learn

SCRIPTURAL BACKGROUND

The Bible records that on the night of His arrest, Jesus was led away to the high priest and an assembly of the chief priests, the elders, and the scribes (Mark 14:53). His dear friend and apostle, Peter, was following behind at a safe distance. Peter had followed into the high priest's courtyard and was warming himself near the fire the servants had prepared (Mark 14:54). This was where Peter would soon deny the promised Messiah of whom Moses and the prophets had written (John 1:45).

Just hours before, Peter had witnessed Judas the betrayer leading a great crowd of men with swords and clubs to arrest Jesus (Mark 14:43). Peter had courageously drawn his sword to fight back—and cut off the ear of one of the men (Mark 14:47). (It is interesting to note that the doctor, Luke, is the only Gospel writer to record that Jesus miraculously healed this man's ear [Luke 22:51].)

Now, here at the fire, in the night, Peter was recognized by one of the servant girls. She accused him of being with Jesus. But he quickly denied it. This denial was accompanied by the first of two rooster crows. Again, the servant girl saw him and charged Peter that he had been with Jesus. Once more, Peter quickly denied this charge. Later, those standing nearby looked at Peter and claimed that his Galilean speech gave him away—he WAS a disciple of Jesus. And a third time, Peter denied His Lord with cursing and swearing that he did not know the one who had been arrested. Just then Peter heard the rooster crow the second time and was reminded of Jesus's warning that Peter would very soon deny Him three times

(Mark 14:66–71). And in the midst of this final denial, the Lord turned and looked at Peter (Luke 22:61).

What a look that must have been! The Master looked on His servant—the one who had declared just hours before that even if all the others left Jesus, he never would (Mark 14:29). Many believe this look was not a look of anger but of tenderness, sorrow, and pity. This loving look from Jesus brought Peter to conviction, humility, and repentance, and he immediately went out and wept bitterly (Luke 22:62).

In the next few days Jesus would be falsely accused, crucified, and then resurrected from the grave. We can only imagine Peter's anguish as the events of the crucifixion played, out and he remembered his last testimony about his Savior—"I do not know this Man of whom you speak!" (Mark 14:71).

Shortly after His resurrection, the Bible tells us that Jesus appeared to the disciples on three different occasions (John 20:19, 20:26, 21:4). During the third visit with His disciples, Jesus directly addressed Peter. It is during this conversation that Jesus asked Peter to confirm his love for His Savior. Jesus did not ask once, but three times, "Simon, son of Jonah, do you love Me?" (John 21:15– 17). Many believe that by repeating His question three times, Jesus was reminding Peter of the three times he had denied even knowing Jesus, just days before. This time, Peter answered earnestly, "Yes, Lord; You know that I love You" (John 21:15).

Jesus's response to Peter was one of forgiveness and confidence in his friend whose faith had recently faltered out of weakness and fear. This confidence was exhibited once again when, three times, Jesus said to Peter, "Feed My lambs"

(John 21:15); "Tend My sheep" (John 21:16); "Feed My sheep" (John 21:17). This was no easy task Jesus had called Peter to. But Peter had once and for all verified his love and loyalty to the Lord. In return the Lord presented him with the privilege of leading others and guiding them into the spiritual truths they would continue to need after Jesus's ascension.

Peter had denied Christ three times. Jesus then gave Peter the opportunity to proclaim his love for Christ three times. After that Jesus commissioned Peter to go and "feed the lambs" three times. This charge and the responsibility that went with it left no doubt that Peter had been forgiven and restored as an ambassador for Jesus Christ.

HISTORICAL/APOLOGETICS BACKGROUND

When reading of the failings of Peter, we might be tempted to say, "How could he do that? If I had been there, I would not have denied Christ!" We ask ourselves, "How could a follower of Jesus—someone who walked with Jesus, witnessed His miracles, and heard His powerful teaching—deny even knowing Him?" Well, Peter gives us a profound lesson in the danger of self-confidence.

Peter had his moments of brilliance, like when he answered Jesus's inquiry about who He was. "You are the Christ, the Son of the living God" was Peter's reply. And Jesus told Peter that it was not by his own wisdom that he knew this, but God had revealed the truth to Peter (Matthew 16:13–17). Another time, after some hard sayings of Jesus, many of His disciples no longer followed Him. Jesus asked the twelve if they also wanted to go away. Peter replied, "Lord, to whom shall we go? You have the words of eternal life. Also we have come to believe and know that

You are the Christ, the Son of the living God" (John 6:66–69).

It seems that Peter, maybe due to some of his successes, had developed a sense of self-confidence. When Jesus predicted His coming crucifixion and that His disciples would stumble, Peter proudly proclaimed, "Even if all are made to stumble, yet I will not be" (Mark 14:27–29). And when Jesus told Peter that Satan had requested to sift him like wheat, but Jesus had prayed that his faith would not fail, Peter boldly retorted, "Lord, I am ready to go with You, both to prison and to death" (Luke 22:31–33). Then, when the soldiers came to arrest Jesus, it was Peter trying to prove his courage and his devotion who drew a sword and whacked off the ear of the servant of the High Priest. In Peter's mind, he was faithful and invincible. But, he was dangerously overconfident.

Just a few hours later, Peter denied knowing Jesus three times. How could this happen? This was Peter, the great leader of the apostles—the one who showed such confidence and boldness! And note that this was not just a momentary slipup, but Peter's denials occurred over a period of two hours. And while the first one may be excusable since he was caught off guard, the next two were most definitely deliberate and premeditated.

While we may criticize Peter for disowning his Lord, if we are honest, we must admit our own failings and our own shortcomings. We may have disowned the Lord, or shrunk back from acknowledging Him, or been afraid to stand up for our faith. And like Peter, we probably felt remorse for our failure.

There was another apostle who denied Jesus, who failed Him, who fell away. This was Judas, the one who betrayed Jesus. Judas, too, felt remorse.

But he went out and hanged himself (Matthew 27:3–5). Peter, instead, wept bitterly, but his faith did not fail. He showed up at the tomb on Sunday. He was in the upper room with the other disciples. Though he failed, he was not destroyed; he persevered in faith. What was the difference between Peter and Judas? Judas was not a true believer in Jesus. Jesus called him a devil, unclean, and the son of perdition (John 6:70–71, 13:10–11, 17:12). Though Judas felt sorrow for his actions, it was not godly sorrow that leads to repentance, but worldly sorrow that leads to death (2 Corinthians 7:10). Peter, on the other hand, was a true believer. His sorrow did lead to repentance and restoration.

In Luke 22, Jesus predicted that Peter would deny Him. But Jesus also said He had prayed for Peter, that his faith would not fail. And Peter's faith did not fail. He stood up on the day of Pentecost and preached a powerful sermon—and 3,000 were converted. Peter continued to preach—and tens of thousands were converted in Jerusalem.

What can we learn from Peter's denials? First of all, we must be very cautious in our self-confidence. We are human; we are frail; we are not exempt from falling into sin or from denying our Lord. The Bible warns us about misplaced self-confidence:

1 Corinthians 10:12 – "Therefore let him who thinks he stands take heed lest he fall."

Galatians 6:1 – "Brethren, if a man is overtaken in any trespass, you who are spiritual restore such a one in a spirit of gentleness, considering yourself lest you also be tempted."

The second thing we can learn from Peter's experience is that God is faithful. As Jesus prayed for Peter's faith not to fail, so He ever lives to intercede for us: "Therefore He is also able to save to the uttermost those who come to God through Him, since He always lives to make intercession for them" (Hebrews 7:25). As Peter was forgiven by Christ, so we, too, can be forgiven as we confess our sins: "If we confess our sins, He is faithful and just to forgive us our sins and to cleanse us from all unrighteousness" (1 John 1:9). God has promised to continue the work He has begun in us. Paul told the believers in Philippi that he was "confident of this very thing, that He who has begun a good work in you will complete it until the day of Jesus Christ" (Philippians 1:6). Praise God that those whom He predestined, called, and justified, He will also glorify (Romans 8:30)!

For more information on this topic, see the Online Resource Page.

 Studying God's Word

How many times do you deny Jesus as Lord in a given week?

_____

Take notes as you study the following passages.

Mark 14:26–31, 14:53–54, 14:66–72

_____

_____

_____

_____

John 21:1–19

_____

_____

_____

_____

 God's Restoring Grace

Follow your teacher's instructions as you complete the God's Restoring Grace worksheet.

 God's Word in the Real World

1. What encouragement do you find in this account of Peter's denial and restoration?

2. What warning do we need to take from Peter's statements of confidence in not stumbling and denying Jesus (consider 1 Corinthians 10:12)?

3. How does the restoration of Peter by Jesus relate to Paul's words in Ephesians 2:10? How does this relate to your life?

4. How can we work together as members of the body of Christ to help keep one another from stumbling and also to promote restoration?

5. How could you use the lesson material today to either encourage a believer who is struggling in his faith or point an unbeliever to the hope of the gospel?

Prayer Requests

_____

_____

_____

_____

_____

_____

_____

4
The Crucifixion

Key Passages

- John 19:17–37; Romans 5:6–9;
  2 Corinthians 5:21; Isaiah 53:1–12

What You Will Learn

- What happened to Jesus on the Cross.
- What was accomplished on the Cross.

Lesson Overview

Jesus was beaten and mocked. A crown of thorns was placed upon His head, and He was told to carry His cross to Golgotha. Nailed to the Cross, Jesus suffered the Father's wrath and paid the penalty for the sin that was laid upon Jesus. Knowing that He had completed the task the Father had sent Him to do, Jesus said, "It is finished," and died.

Memory Verse

Matthew 28:18–20

And Jesus came and spoke to them, saying, "All authority has been given to Me in heaven and on earth. Go therefore and make disciples of all the nations, baptizing them in the name of the Father and of the Son and of the Holy Spirit, teaching them to observe all things that I have commanded you; and lo, I am with you always, even to the end of the age." Amen.

Prepare to Learn

SCRIPTURAL BACKGROUND

The sinless Son of Man had come to seek and to save the lost (Luke 19:10). He would be led like a lamb to the slaughter (Isaiah 53:7). He would not open His mouth but willingly accept and finish the plan the Father had in place since the beginning of time. After the illegal and unjust arrest and conviction of Jesus, He was sentenced to death—crucifixion on the Cross (John 19:16).

At the time, this was one of the most disgraceful and humiliating forms of death. Pilate had Jesus scourged, and He was mockingly crowned with a painful crown of thorns that was pressed into His head (John 19:1–2). In a very weakened state He was led out to carry the very cross He would be nailed to and killed upon. He was headed to Golgotha where the crucifixion would occur (John 19:17). Because of His weakened state, the authorities compelled Simon, a Cyrenian, to assist Jesus with the Cross (Mark 15:21). Jesus was offered wine with myrrh in order to lessen the pain He was about to endure, but He refused it (Mark 15:23). He was nailed through His hands and His feet to the Cross. He was crucified between two criminals (John 19:18). The title Pilate assigned to Him, "King of the Jews" was placed on the Cross (John 19:19). As He hung in agony, soldiers cast lots for His clothes (John 19:23–24), and people shouted insults at Him (Mark 15:29–30). In the midst of all of this, Jesus looked at His mother from the Cross, spoke to her, loved her, and left her in the care of His friend and apostle John (John 19:26–27).

After this, knowing that all things were now accomplished, Jesus said, "I thirst!" This was the final Scripture to be fulfilled (John 19:28).

As Jesus suffered, many heard Him cry out to His Father, "My God, My God, why have You forsaken Me? (Mark 15:34). And finally, as He gave up His spirit, Jesus said, "It is finished" (John 19:30).

Jesus was physically distressed, no doubt. But when He felt that His Father had forsaken Him, this was a distress that went beyond the physical. What did Jesus mean? What was He feeling? It may have been at this point after suffering so immeasurably, knowing that He would soon die, that He also felt the weight and extent of God's wrath on Him for sins He did not, nor could He ever, commit!

In this act of bearing God's wrath upon Himself, Jesus finished the work the Father had sent Him to do; the work of redemption was now complete. The punishment for the sins of everyone who would ever turn to Jesus in repentance and faith had been poured out on the perfect Lamb of God. The debt for sin was paid in full for all who would follow the Lord Jesus Christ.

This is the wonder of the gospel! God demonstrated His own love toward us, in that while we were still sinners, Christ died for us. We are justified by His blood. And because Jesus was willing to take the wrath upon Himself, we shall be saved from the wrath due us for our sin (Romans 5:6–9).

In God's gracious and merciful plan, He made His only Son, Jesus Christ, who knew no sin, to be sin for us. Jesus took the sin, the wrath, and the punishment. In exchange, believers receive the precious righteousness of God that is the very nature of Jesus

Christ and the promise of eternal life with the Father, Son, and Holy Spirit (2 Corinthians 5:21).

As we meditate on the truth of Jesus's death and what it accomplished for sinners who would one day believe, we can see what led the Apostle Paul to declare in his letter to the Romans:

> Oh, the depth of the riches both of the wisdom and knowledge of God!
>
> How unsearchable are His judgments and His ways past finding out!
>
> "For who has known the mind of the Lord? Or who has become His counselor?"
>
> "Or who has first given to Him and it shall be repaid to him?"
>
> For of Him and through Him and to Him are all things, to whom be glory forever. Amen (Romans 11:33–36).

HISTORICAL/APOLOGETICS BACKGROUND

People sometimes ask who killed Jesus. Who was responsible for His death? Was it the Romans, the Jewish leaders, the Jewish people? The answer is yes . . . and more.

Certainly, the Jewish leaders had a hand in Jesus's Crucifixion. God tells us in His Word that it was the chief priests, the scribes, and the elders of the people who plotted to take Jesus by trickery and kill Him (Matthew 26:3–4). The Jewish leaders demanded that Jesus be killed rather than the criminal Barabbas (Matthew 27:20). The power and reputation of Jesus threatened these Jewish leaders. They felt compelled to be rid of Him and plotted His death (John 11:47–50, 11:53).

The people of Israel also participated in the death of Jesus as they shouted, "Crucify Him! Crucify Him!" during His trial (Luke 23:21).

However, in the end, it was the Romans, under the authority of the governor, Pontius Pilate, who actually authorized the Crucifixion. Jesus's death was physically carried out by Roman soldiers, who erected the Cross, drove the nails into His hands and feet, and pierced His side (Matthew 27:27–37).

This corporate responsibility for Jesus's death is confirmed in Scripture. It was Herod, Pilate, the Gentiles, and the people of Israel together who cooperated to kill Jesus (Acts 4:27). And this was an unusual conspiracy as these groups were often at odds with one another, but united together to murder the Savior. And let us not forget that we, too, caused the Savior's death. It was our sin for which He died.

But that is not the only answer to the question of who killed Jesus. As we search God's Word, we will come to understand that, amazingly, the death of Jesus Christ was ordained and accomplished by the determined purpose and foreknowledge of God Himself (Acts 2:23, 4:28).

The prophet Isaiah spoke of Christ's torture and death nearly 700 years before it occurred. And Isaiah wrote that it pleased the Lord to bruise Him and put Him to grief. God's plan had always been that His Son's soul would be an offering for sin (Isaiah 53:10).

In what sense did it please the Lord? God the Father was pleased that His eternal plan of salvation was fulfilled (Ephesians 1:4). He was pleased that the death of his Son would bring eternal life to many (Matthew 1:21). He was pleased to demonstrate His love for sinners through such a magnificent sacrifice (Romans 5:8).

Yes, it ultimately was God Himself who determined, before the foundation of the world (1 Peter 1:20; Revelation 13:8), to send His Son to live a perfect life, to die, and to be raised again from the dead so that sinners could be forgiven. In fact, this would be the ONLY possible way sinners could be reconciled to the holy, perfect, righteous God.

And yet, here lies the paradox—the tension between man's responsibility and God's sovereignty. For in spite of God's pre-determination of Christ's death, each man will be held responsible for the role he played in completing God's plan. It was still an act of "lawless hands" as Peter said (Acts 2:23). And Jesus Himself said He must go as had been determined, but woe to the one who betrayed Him (Luke 22:22).

The death of God the Son—Jesus Christ—on the Cross is undoubtedly the most horrific sin ever committed. And yet in it, we see the absolute sovereignty of God. In spite of the evil perpetrated, God's infinitely good and eternal plan was perfectly fulfilled. The Cross shows us more clearly than anything else that God's perfect purposes will be accomplished in spite of, and even through, the evil intentions of sinners (Romans 8:28).

We cannot leave the topic of the Crucifixion—and who was responsible for it—without a careful examination of our own hearts. We who have come to faith in Christ are also guilty of His blood, shed on the Cross for us. He died to pay the penalty for our sins (Romans 5:8, 6:23). Therefore, we should live in way that shows gratitude for what Jesus has done. He has redeemed us by His precious blood (1 Peter 1:18–19). He bore our sins in His own body on the tree that we might die to sin and live to righteousness. By His wounds we have been healed (1 Peter 2:24–25).

If you belong to Christ, you may rejoice! For this is an amazing plan of God—that through the perfect life and death of Jesus Christ, He who knew no sin became sin for us, that we might become the righteousness of God in Him (2 Corinthians 5:21). Oh, what a Savior we serve! And what hope we have in Him!

For more information on this topic, see the Online Resource Page.

 # Studying God's Word

What was accomplished on the Cross?

_____

_____

Take notes as you study the following passages.

John 19:16–37

_____

_____

_____

Isaiah 53:1–12

_____

_____

_____

Romans 5:6–11

_____

_____

_____

2 Corinthians 5:12–21

_____

_____

_____

 A Prophetic Death

For each of the Old Testament passages below, provide a short description of what was predicted and how it came to fulfillment in the Crucifixion. If you can, identify the passage in the New Testament that describes the fulfillment.

- Psalm 22:1

- Psalm 22:6–8

- Psalm 22:16

- Psalm 22:18

- Psalm 69:21

- Zechariah 12:10

- Isaiah 53:5

- Isaiah 53:11

God's Word in the Real World

1. Knowing that all of the suffering Jesus faced on the Cross was part of God's plan before time began and was prophesied throughout the Old Testament, has there ever been a more loving act done for you?

2. How could you incorporate the love demonstrated by Jesus on the Cross to encourage believers and call unbelievers to trust in Christ?

3. It seems almost blasphemous, but Scripture says that it pleased the Father to crush His Son (Isaiah 53:10; Acts 2:22–24). How can we explain this in a way that is consistent with God's character?

4. While God was ultimately in control over the death of Jesus, in what way are you and I responsible for the death of Jesus?

5. If Jesus died on the Cross, and His work is finished, what does this mean about our own efforts to cover our sins?

6. The prophecies of Jesus's Crucifixion are not something that can be easily ignored. How can these prophecies be used with believers and unbelievers?

Prayer Requests

The Resurrection

5

Key Passages

- Matthew 28:1–10; John 11:25–26, 14:19; 1 Peter 1:3–9

What You Will Learn

- What happened at Jesus's tomb after His death.

- Why Jesus's Resurrection was necessary to secure our redemption.

Lesson Overview

The women went to Jesus's tomb early on Sunday morning. They found the stone to the tomb rolled away, the tomb empty, and an angel of the Lord there. The angel told them Jesus was risen from the dead. On their way to tell the disciples, they saw Jesus and worshipped Him. Jesus's Resurrection from the dead is important because it provides an inheritance for believers—a living hope—eternal life with God.

Memory Verse

Matthew 28:18–20

And Jesus came and spoke to them, saying, "All authority has been given to Me in heaven and on earth. Go therefore and make disciples of all the nations, baptizing them in the name of the Father and of the Son and of the Holy Spirit, teaching them to observe all things that I have commanded you; and lo, I am with you always, even to the end of the age." Amen.

📖 Prepare to Learn

SCRIPTURAL BACKGROUND

Jesus lived His life and died according God's plan ordained before the foundation of the world (Ephesians 1:4). On the Cross, Jesus finished the work the Father had sent Him to do. He bore God's wrath on Himself and took the punishment for the sins of everyone who would ever turn in repentance and faith to Him.

But there was still more to come—the glorious event that brought assurance to the stunning truth that sinners would have eternal life with God (John 5:24; Romans 5:18)! This event is the Resurrection of Jesus from the grave (Matthew 28). What happened on that victorious morning?

We know that Joseph of Arimathea had taken the body of Jesus and laid it in a new tomb. A large stone was rolled against the door (Matthew 27:59–60). The tomb was sealed, and a guard was placed at the entrance (Matthew 27:66). The Bible tells us that two women came to the tomb at dawn. There had been a great earthquake and an angel of the Lord had appeared from heaven and rolled the stone away from the door. Now the angel sat upon it (Matthew 28:1–2). This was the messenger from God. He announced that the Savior, who had been crucified, had risen just as He said He would. The women were instructed to go and tell the disciples this amazing news (Matthew 28:5–7).

As though this were not enough good news for one morning, the women then encountered Jesus Christ Himself! He told them to "Rejoice!" and "Do not be afraid. Go and tell My brethren to go to Galilee, and there they will see me" (Matthew 28:9–10).

What is the significance of this miraculous event? The Apostle Paul understood what it meant, and understood the importance of believing it is true. You see, Paul tells us that if Christ is not risen then our faith and our preaching is empty. And there would be NO resurrection to eternal life for believers (1 Corinthians 15:12–15). He states that if Christ is not risen, our faith is futile, we are not forgiven, but still in our sins. If Christ is not alive, we are to be pitied because without the Resurrection our hope in Christ does not exceed the boundaries of our life here on earth (1 Corinthians 15:17–19).

But believers are not to be pitied. We believe that Jesus did rise from the dead. And with that belief comes an amazing promise and assurance. The Bible tells us that the risen Jesus Christ has destroyed the last enemy—death (1 Corinthians 15:26)! Jesus IS the resurrection and the life. Those who believe in Him will live even though they die (John 11:25). This is our hope. It is a living hope promised through the mercy of God in Jesus Christ through His resurrection from the dead. This precious hope guarantees an inheritance in heaven that will not fade away (1 Peter 1:3–5).

The Resurrection is a critical part of the gospel. Christ died for sins according to the Scriptures, and He was buried and rose again according to the Scriptures (1 Corinthians 15:3–4). Everyone who has turned away from their sins in repentance and faith and turned to the risen Jesus Christ for forgiveness will have the hope of eternal life. Jesus alone is the Savior, the Redeemer, the Lord. He alone is life and brings life. He is risen! He is alive! And because

He lives, we who are in Christ, will live also (John 14:19).

The wonder of the Resurrection brings to mind a hymn written in 1757 by Christian F. Gellers.

Jesus lives, and so shall I, Death!
Thy sting is gone forever.

He who deigned for me to die,
lives, the bands of death to sever.

He shall raise me with the just:
Jesus is my hope and trust.

HISTORICAL/APOLOGETICS BACKGROUND

The bodily Resurrection of Jesus Christ is the most significant event in history. The Apostle Paul always included the Resurrection as a vital part of the gospel he had preached (1 Corinthians 15:1–4). It is a doctrine that brings hope and joy. Let's look at some of the reasons for that.

First, the Resurrection of Jesus provides indisputable evidence that He is who He claimed to be—the Son of God, God in the flesh. Paul affirmed that Christ was "declared to be the Son of God with power . . . by the resurrection from the dead" (Romans 1:4).

Second, the Resurrection not only validated Jesus's claim to Deity but also proved His teachings to be true. He claimed many times that He would be raised on the third day (John 2:19–21; Mark 8:31, 9:31, 10:34). And His Resurrection confirmed what He said to be true.

Third, the Resurrection validated Jesus's sacrificial death. Jesus died for sinners, and His Resurrection and victory over death shows that God accepted the sacrifice as payment in full.

As mentioned above, the Apostle Paul clearly understood the significance of Christ's bodily Resurrection. In 1 Corinthians 15 Paul gives six devastating consequences that would occur if Christ was not raised bodily from the grave: 1) preaching Christ would be pointless (v. 14); 2) our faith in Christ would be empty (v. 14); 3) all those who have testified to the Resurrection would be liars (v. 15); 4) no one would be redeemed from sin (v. 17); 5) all who had died would have perished because they would have died in their sins (v.18); and 6) Christians would be the most pitiable people on the earth (v. 19).

Fourth, Jesus's Resurrection proves that physical death is not the end of human existence. It points forward to the resurrection of human beings, which is a core doctrine of the Christian faith. God, who gives life to all things (1 Timothy 6:13), has the power to resurrect the human body. Christ's triumph over the grave is God's pledge to us that we, too, shall be raised, as the Apostle Paul stated:

But now Christ is risen from the dead, and has become the firstfruits of those who have fallen asleep. For since by man came death, by Man also came the resurrection of the dead. For as in Adam all die, even so in Christ all shall be made alive. But each one in his own order: Christ the firstfruits, afterward those who are Christ's at His coming." (1 Corinthians 15:20–23).

Fifth, the Resurrection tells the world that the kingdom of God is ruled by a living sovereign who has accomplished redemption, not through the works of men, but through the gift of grace through faith (Ephesians 2:8). Unlike all other religions, Christianity alone is led by one who has defeated death and who promises that His followers will do the same. The founders of all other religions are in the grave; they are dead and gone. Christ alone is alive! As the risen Savior, about 60 years after His death, said to the Apostle John: "I am the First and the Last. I am He who lives, and was dead, and behold, I am alive forevermore. Amen" (Revelation 1:17–18).

Jesus Christ came to make a way for sinners to get to heaven. He offered Himself as the perfect sacrifice—to make atonement for the sins of all believers (2 Corinthians 5:21). How do we know His sacrifice was sufficient? Because of the mystery of the Resurrection. God raised Him from the grave and seated Him at His right hand (Romans 8:34)! Believers have been justified in the eyes of God because our Savior is alive! And God assures us in His Word that those He [Jesus] justified, these He also glorified (Romans 8:30).

The future resurrection of believers is our blessed hope. Jesus Christ died, was buried, and rose on the third day according to the Scriptures. This is something we are to celebrate—not just once a year, but every day! Believers are born again to a living hope through His Resurrection (1 Peter 1:3). Because He lives, all believers will also live (John 14:19). The will of God the Father is accomplished. Everyone who looks on the Son and believes in Him will have eternal life. And God will raise them up on the last day (John 6:40).

Because Jesus is alive, we can be confident that He will come again to receive His children to Himself (John 14:3)! And what a glorious day that will be! The dead in Christ will be raised up, and those who remain and are alive at His coming will be changed and receive new, glorified bodies (1 Thessalonians 4:13–18; 1 Corinthians 15:51–52). All because Jesus Christ is risen from the dead!

For more information on this topic, see the Online Resource Page.

 ## Studying God's Word

What did the Resurrection accomplish?

_____

_____

Take notes as you study the following passage.

Matthew 28:1–10

_____

_____

_____

_____

_____

 ## A Risen Savior

When we think about sharing the gospel, we almost always think of Christ's work on the Cross. However, as we examine the New Testament, there is another element that is included. Read the following passages and write a short summary of the role of the Resurrection in each passage. Then, answer the questions that follow.

- Acts 2:22–36

- Acts 3:11–16

- Acts 4:8–12

- Romans 4:23–25

- 1 Corinthians 15:1–5, 15:12–19

- 2 Corinthians 5:14–16

1. What is the connection in these passages between the death and the Resurrection of Jesus in presenting the gospel?

2. Do you always mention both the Cross and the Resurrection when you share the gospel?

3. Considering Paul's words in 1 Corinthians 2:1–5, if you don't remember to mention the Resurrection in a presentation of the gospel, have you failed to offer the hope of Christ for salvation?

Take notes as you study the following passage.

1 Peter 1:3–9

_____

_____

_____

_____

_____

⊕ God's Word in the Real World

1. How has your understanding of the necessity of the Resurrection changed over time (or through this lesson)?

2. What is your favorite song that reminds you of the hope of eternal life found in Christ's Resurrection?

3. How does the doctrine of the Resurrection set Christianity apart from other religious ideas? How can we use that in evangelistic endeavors?

4. To be considered a Christian, why is it absolutely necessary to confess that Jesus rose bodily from the dead?

5. In two weeks we will look in detail at some of the ways skeptics try to deny the Resurrection, but what is the primary tool we should use to refute the claims of those who deny that Jesus rose from the dead?

Prayer Requests

The Great Commission

6

Key Passages

*   Matthew 28:18–20; Romans 1:16–17,
    10:14–17

What You Will Learn

*   The purpose of the Great Commission.

*   Who is responsible for fulfilling the Great
    Commission.

Lesson Overview

Jesus's last command to His followers was that they preach the gospel and make disciples of all nations. All believers share in that same responsibility and are called to go to all nations with the gospel of truth. This is important because the gospel is the good news, and it alone can bring eternal life.

Memory Verse

Matthew 28:18–20

And Jesus came and spoke to them, saying, "All authority has been given to Me in heaven and on earth. Go therefore and make disciples of all the nations, baptizing them in the name of the Father and of the Son and of the Holy Spirit, teaching them to observe all things that I have commanded you; and lo, I am with you always, even to the end of the age." Amen.

 **Prepare to Learn**

SCRIPTURAL BACKGROUND

Jesus Christ was delivered up according to the determined purpose of God. He was crucified, put to death, and then raised from the dead (Acts 2:23–24). Through His Resurrection, Jesus destroyed the final enemy—that is death (1 Corinthians 15:26). Now those who believe in Him shall never die (John 11:26).

Jesus appeared to His followers after His Resurrection. In fact, the Bible records no less than ten times that Jesus was seen after He rose. He showed Himself alive by many infallible proofs (Acts 1:3). The Apostle Paul summarized some of these appearances when He wrote that Jesus was seen by Cephas, then by the twelve, then by over 500 hundred, then by James, and then by all the apostles (1 Corinthians 15:3–7).

For 40 days Jesus continued to show Himself, teach, and prepare His followers for life without His physical presence. When it finally came time for Him to return to His Father, He gave His parting instructions. This is what is now known as the Great Commission. What was Jesus's message?

He began by once again confirming His authority—ALL authority has been given to Him in heaven and on earth (Matthew 28:18). He was crucified for claiming He was God (John 10:30–31). And this statement declared His claim to be true! Jesus the Messiah is the Great I AM (John 8:58). He is Lord over the entire universe.

He then told His followers to "make disciples." This is a call that includes evangelism—proclaiming the gospel to others—as well as teaching and guiding these disciples to observe all that Jesus commanded (Matthew 28:20). And this is a commission to ALL believers through the ages. How critical it is that we obey it. We know that everyone who calls on the name of the Lord will be saved (Romans 10:13). But how will anyone call on the Lord if they do not believe in Him? And how will they believe in Him if they have not heard of Him (Romans 10:14)? We must proclaim the truth to unbelievers. The Bible tells us that faith comes by hearing, and hearing by the Word of God (Romans 10:17). We are to be bold and not ashamed of the gospel. It is the gospel that is the power of God to salvation for everyone who believes (Romans 1:16). Without the truth of the gospel, people will perish in their sins.

Jesus told His followers to baptize the disciples in the name of the Father, the Son, and the Holy Spirit (Matthew 28:19.) This external baptism by water is a picture of what happens when a person trusts in Christ. They die with Christ, are buried with Christ, and are raised to newness of life (Romans 6:4).

Scripture also talks about another baptism. This baptism comes through the Holy Spirit to all believers who are united with Christ through faith in the gospel. This is an internal baptism by which the Holy Spirit makes believers new creations in Christ Jesus (2 Corinthians 5:17). It is often referred to as being "born again" by the Holy Spirit (John 3:6–7). This baptism seals believers with the Holy Spirit of promise assuring them that they are guaranteed the inheritance that Christ purchased to the praise of the glory of God (Ephesians 2:13–14)!

And the Great Commission does not stop there! It continues beyond a new believer's repentance and faith. You see, a new Christian is like a newborn—unskilled in the word of righteousness (Hebrews 5:13). There is a new life in their soul, with amazing potential to learn and grow in wisdom and knowledge of the truth. These new believers are to be molded by the truth and trained to do all that Jesus commanded (Matthew 28:20). Those older and more mature in the faith are to instruct the younger Christians so they will continue to grow and bear fruit for the Lord (Titus 2:3; 2 Timothy 2:2).

Jesus ended His Great Commission with a promise that gives the encouragement and strength necessary to boldly fulfill His command. He told His disciples, and He tells us, "Lo! I am with you always, even to the end of the age." We can be assured and confident of this promise as we strive to fulfill the Great Commission in our own lives.

HISTORICAL/APOLOGETICS BACKGROUND

If you've ever been to a missionary conference, no doubt the Great Commission was read aloud or written on a banner. This is the church's marching orders—to make disciples of all nations. Sometimes we think that this was a new idea that Jesus instituted, when in reality, God's heart has always been for the nations. God's covenant with Israel in the Old Testament wasn't for their sake alone. No, God had always intended that Israel would be a light to the nations (Isaiah 42:6, 49:6, 60:3). As we look at the Old Testament, there are many clear passages that show this to be true.

As early as Genesis, God's intent to use the nation of Israel as a catalyst to spread His Word to all the world is clear. The judgment for the Tower of Babel scattered people across the earth, and nations were formed. This was followed by God's promise to Abram that through him and his seed "all the families of the earth shall be blessed" (Genesis 12:3). God would use Abraham, the father of Israel, in a way that would be a means of blessing all the nations; from his seed, Jesus Christ would come and provide redemption to the world. This promise of worldwide blessing was later restated to Abraham: "In your seed all the nations of the earth shall be blessed, because you have obeyed my voice" (Genesis 18:18, 22:18). The same promise was then given to Isaac (Genesis 26:4) and then to Jacob as the father of the 12 tribes of Israel (Genesis 28:14). The world would be blessed through Abraham's seed.

God's desire and heart was not just for Israel. But He would use Israel, and His Word to them, to proclaim truth across the earth. We see in many of the psalms that all nations would be included in the praise and worship of the Lord God of Israel. One in particular is Psalm 67. The universal nature of this psalm proclaims that God's way will be known on ALL the earth and His salvation among ALL nations (Psalm 67:2). The psalmist goes on to plead that ALL the peoples will praise God, that ALL the nations will be glad and sing for joy (Psalm 67:3–4)!

We know that Israel was God's chosen nation. And yet God was jealous for all the peoples of the earth—both Jews and Gentiles—that they would worship His name. It is hard to miss the many Gentiles God spoke of in the Old Testament. These men and women were known to be followers of the one true God of Israel. We encounter people like Melchizedek, the king of Salem (Genesis 14:18); Jethro of Midian, Moses's father-in-law (Exodus 3:1); Rahab, the harlot in Jericho (Joshua 2:1); Ruth of Moab (Ruth 1:4); the widow of Zarephath (1 Kings 17:9); and many others like them. These people from many nations responded to the good news of God's reign. And who can forget God sending Jonah to take the message of repentance to the cruel Assyrians of Nineveh? The people of that pagan city believed God, repented of their sins, and turned to the one, true, holy God (Jonah 3:5–10).

You see, God did not ordain that Israel alone would receive the blessing of salvation through the Messiah. No, God called Israel and put her into service to spread His name to the nations of the earth. The decisive fulfillment of God's covenant with Abraham—that the nations of the earth would be blessed through his seed—was accomplished in the life, death, and Resurrection of Jesus Christ, the "seed of Abraham." God's plan was that through Jesus Christ ALL people—including those from the most pagan nations—can become sons of Abraham and heirs of all his blessings through faith in Jesus Christ.

So when Jesus left His followers with the Great Commission, He was continuing the purpose of His Father that the everlasting gospel would be preached to those who dwell on the earth—to every nation, tribe, tongue, and people—that they would fear God and give Him glory, and that they would forever worship Him who made heaven and earth (Revelation 5:9–10).

Now and always, Christians have the great privilege and the solemn responsibility to take the message of the gospel to the nations of the world. Matthew 28:18–20 is not called the Great Suggestion, but the Great Commission. May we be found faithful.

For more information on this topic, see the Online Resource Page.

 **Studying God's Word**

Are you obeying the Great Commission?

_____

Take notes as you study the following passage.

Matthew 28:18–20

_____

_____

_____

_____

_____

 **Whose Commission?**

Answer the following questions.

1. Do you believe that you are responsible to spread the good news of the gospel as an evangelist? Why or why not?

2. In Matthew 28:18–20, the disciples were commanded to spread the gospel, make disciples, and to teach those disciples all that Jesus had taught them. If Jesus taught the disciples to spread the gospel, would the new disciples be responsible for spreading the gospel, too?

3. In Luke 24:46–48, Jesus addressed the disciples. To whom were they to preach the gospel? Is this possible for this small group of disciples who lived nearly 2,000 years ago?

4. In 2 Corinthians 5:18–21, what role do those who have been reconciled in Christ have?

5. How has your answer to the first question changed in light of these passages?

6. What hinders you most from being bold as an ambassador of Jesus Christ and His gospel?

Take notes as you study the following passage.

Romans 1:15–17, 10:9–17

_____

_____

_____

_____

_____

God's Word in the Real World

1. How would the world be different if the Great Commission had not been carried on by the generation that followed the original 12 disciples?

2. In what ways has your thinking about the responsibility of evangelism changed over time, and what influenced that thinking?

3. We have all had fears about sharing the gospel with others. How can we overcome these fears and seek to be obedient as witnesses of Jesus?

4. Have you ever found a new recipe or a new app that you just loved and had to tell everyone about? How does this example relate to our proclamation of the gospel?

5. What should be the supreme motivator in fulfilling the Great Commission?

6. How could adopting the following phrase encourage us to obey the Great Commission: "I am responsible to proclaim the good news, not for the response of the people hearing it"?

Prayer Requests

Resurrection Theories

7

Key Passage

- 1 Corinthians 15:3–28

What You Will Learn

- Several of the common theories skeptics use to discredit the Resurrection.
- Biblical refutations to the false theories of the Resurrection.

Lesson Overview

This week you will watch a video describing some of the false theories that have been invented to discredit the Resurrection, and how we can be assured that the Resurrection of Jesus Christ from the dead is a fact of history.

Memory Verse

Matthew 28:18–20

And Jesus came and spoke to them, saying, "All authority has been given to Me in heaven and on earth. Go therefore and make disciples of all the nations, baptizing them in the name of the Father and of the Son and of the Holy Spirit, teaching them to observe all things that I have commanded you; and lo, I am with you always, even to the end of the age." Amen.

SCRIPTURAL BACKGROUND

There can be no doubt in our minds that the Resurrection is one of the core doctrines of the Christian faith. Jesus Himself talked about the necessity of His Resurrection to the disciples. Luke records Jesus saying, "Thus it is written, and thus it was necessary for the Christ to suffer and to rise from the dead the third day, and that repentance and remission of sins should be preached in His name to all nations, beginning at Jerusalem. And you are witnesses of these things" (Luke 24:46–48). Notice that in saying, "Thus it is written" Jesus was referring to what was written before. And what was that? The Old Testament—the only Scriptures available at the time. God had planned from the beginning of time that Jesus would die for sinners and be raised to life on the third day. The Resurrection of Christ was just as necessary in the mind and decrees of God as the death of Christ was (1 Corinthians 15:3–5).

So, where do we see the Resurrection alluded to in the Old Testament? First, it is important to recall that all of the Old Testament was pointing forward to the coming of the Messiah. The thread of redemption is seen there as early as Genesis 3:15, where Christ's ultimate victory over Satan is prophesied.

Peter recited Psalm 16:10 as he preached on the Day of Pentecost (Acts 2:31). He was confirming that the writer of Psalm 16 was referring not only to David, but to Jesus Christ, the Son of David, and His Resurrection from the dead.

It appears that even the historical account of Jonah who was swallowed by a fish and left there for three days and three nights was a foreshadowing of the death, burial, and Resurrection of Jesus Christ. Jesus Himself referred to this account as He explained to the Pharisees that just as Jonah was three days and three nights in the belly of the great fish, so would the Son of Man [Jesus] be three days and three night in the heart of the earth (Matthew 12:39–40).

The Resurrection showed clearly that Jesus Christ had the power to destroy death—the last enemy (1 Corinthians 15:26). This realization made the enemies of God shudder at the truth of the Resurrection of Jesus. But what could they do now that Jesus was alive again? The only thing they could do is seek to discredit the Resurrection. And that they quickly did. The Bible tells us that the chief priests and elders agreed to give a large sum of money to the soldiers who had been guarding the tomb. This was to fund the lie that Jesus's disciples had come at night and stole the body of Jesus while the guards slept (Matthew 28:11–15). From that first week after His death even to this day, those who refuse to submit to the Lordship of Christ have invented many arguments to try and explain away the Resurrection of Jesus from the dead.

HISTORICAL/APOLOGETICS BACKGROUND

While the Bible speaks of Jesus showing Himself by many infallible proofs (Acts 1:3), we must acknowledge that we do not have tangible access to those proofs today. We cannot place our hands in the wounds of the resurrected Savior (John 20:27).

We cannot sit beside the resurrected Jesus and join Him for breakfast (John 21:11–14). We know none of the eye-witnesses who saw and spoke with the resurrected Jesus (1 Corinthians 15:5). But we have a more reliable account to depend on. What we have is the record of all these things and more in the inspired, inerrant Word of God. We can trust all of God's Word, including the accounts of the Resurrection.

Some it seems cannot be convinced or persuaded to believe the truth of the gospel. And Jesus Himself mentioned in the account of the rich man and Lazarus, that unbelievers will not be "persuaded" even though one would rise from the dead (Luke 16:3). Belief in Jesus Christ comes through the witness of Scripture and the illumination of the Holy Spirit and not from convincing arguments. To believe that Jesus is the Son of God, that He bore God's wrath for sin on the Cross, and that He rose victorious over death so that all who place their trust in Him will also be resurrected to eternal life requires more than a convincing argument or intellectual agreement to historical facts. No, belief in Jesus Christ and the Word of God comes through a heart changed by faith through grace (Ephesians 2:8). The Apostle Paul knew this and witnessed it frequently as he travelled and shared to good news of Jesus Christ—His life, death, and Resurrection. He spoke to many, and was only too aware that the message of the Cross was foolishness to those who are perishing, but to those who are being saved, that message is the power of God for salvation (1 Corinthians 1:18).

This does not mean that answering legitimate questions from those who are skeptical of the Resurrection is improper. Dan Barker, president of the Freedom from Religion Foundation and a skeptic, wrote the following about the Resurrection:

> There have been many reasons for doubting the claim, but the consensus among critical scholars today appears to be that the story is a "legend." During the 60–70 years it took for the Gospels to be composed, the original story went through a growth period that began with the unadorned idea that Jesus, like Grandma, had "died and gone to heaven" and ended with a fantastic narrative produced by a later generation of believers that included earthquakes, angels, an eclipse, a resuscitated corpse, and a spectacular bodily ascension into the clouds. The earliest Christians believed in the "spiritual" resurrection of Jesus. The story evolved over time into a "bodily" resurrection. (Dan Barker, "Did Jesus Really Rise from the Dead?" https://ffrf.org/legacy/about/bybarker/rise.php)

This is one objection to the biblical account of the Resurrection. And there are others. For example, it has been said that the person on the Cross was not Jesus. Muslims often claim that Judas took Jesus's place on the Cross and was taken to heaven based on Surah 4:157–158 in the Quran. Consequently, according to the Muslims, if Jesus never died, He was surely never resurrected. But even the text of the Quran is self-refuting since it claims that the Jews were boasting that they killed the Messiah. And though the Jews were responsible for Jesus's death, they never believed He was the Messiah—for no Jew would have killed anyone he considered to be Messiah.

In another source, the Gospel of Barnabas, it is claimed that Judas appeared and the disciples thought it was Jesus. However, this work is considered a false gospel (pseudepigrapha), and the earliest manuscripts are from the 1500s. While some did not recognize Jesus after the Resurrection, the Bible makes it clear that He appeared to many.

Another common rejection is to either deny that Jesus ever existed or to say the teachings on the Resurrection were developed later as mythical components of the spreading of the Christian teachings. But this explanation is problematic because there is no serious scholar who rejects that Jesus actually existed (though they reject He is God), and the manuscript evidence does not support such a claim, with the Resurrection being described in the earliest of writings from the church fathers.Another claim by skeptics is that Jesus just appeared to die on the Cross, so there really wasn't a resurrection, just a reviving of a wounded man. Well, let's think about that. Jesus was scourged, hung on a cross for six hours, had a spear thrust into His chest, was buried in a tomb behind a giant rock, and then walked out of the tomb a few days later, not looking any worse for the wear, and convinced His disciples that He was the resurrected Lord of glory. Ideas like this just show the desperation of those who want to reject Jesus as Lord and Savior, attempting to disprove His Resurrection to do so.

Other ideas such as a mass hallucination, a séance, an apparition, or spirit, appearing to the disciples, and even alien visitations are all attempts to suppress the truth of the Resurrection and the lordship of Christ.

These dismissals of God's Word should be addressed. And often, the objections are not even difficult to answer if we are prepared and familiar with the different opinions we may be confronted with. However, we must keep in mind that in many of these cases, the skeptics will accept a few scraps of evidence for a pagan god, and will not accept the truthfulness of the Bible.

As believers, we should rejoice that God has revealed the truth to those of us who are being saved (1 Corinthians 1:18). And with that divine revelation of the truth comes the privilege and responsibility to open our Bibles and proclaim that "truly, these times of ignorance God overlooked, but now commands all men everywhere to repent, because He has appointed a day on which He will judge the world in righteousness by the Man whom He has ordained. He has given assurance of this to all by raising Him from the dead" (Acts 17:30–31).

For more information on this topic, see the Online Resource Page.

# Studying God's Word

Can we really believe that Jesus rose from the dead?

_____

_____

Resurrection Theories Video

As you watch the video, use the space below to make notes about the various theories that have been proposed to discredit the Resurrection.

_____

_____

_____

_____

_____

_____

_____

_____

_____

Take notes as you study the following passage.

1 Corinthians 15:3–28

_____

_____

_____

God's Word in the Real World

1. If you have ever had some of the doubts about the Resurrection that were expressed in the video today, what was it that helped relieve those doubts?

2. As we consider all of the other religious leaders (Buddha, Muhammad, Joseph Smith, etc.), how does the Resurrection distinguish Christianity from those false systems?

3. Which of the theories described in the video have you had difficulty answering in the past, and how have you been equipped to answer?

4. Why is it important that we never set aside the Bible when we are discussing the truthfulness of the Resurrection with skeptics?

5. If we get caught up in the details of arguing about the Resurrection, how could we miss the importance of communicating the gospel?

Prayer Requests

_____

_____

_____

_____

The Promised Helper Comes

8

Key Passages

- John 16:5–15; Acts 2:1–24; Ephesians 1:13–14; Galatians 5:22–23

What You Will Learn

- How Jesus's promise of the Holy Spirit was fulfilled.

- Explain the work of the Holy Spirit in believers.

Lesson Overview

The Holy Spirit came to the disciples while they were waiting in Jerusalem. They were transformed and empowered by Him. Believers today receive the seal of the Holy Spirit when they are saved. The fruit of the Spirit is evidence that the believer is a new creation in Christ.

Memory Verse

Romans 1:16–17

For I am not ashamed of the gospel of Christ, for it is the power of God to salvation for everyone who believes, for the Jew first and also for the Greek. For in it the righteousness of God is revealed from faith to faith; as it is written, "The just shall live by faith."

 **Prepare to Learn**

SCRIPTURAL BACKGROUND

Before Jesus left this earth to go back to His Father, He left His apostles with one last command. That was to go and preach the gospel, making disciples of all nations, baptizing them and teaching them to observe all things that He commanded (Matthew 28:19–20).

Before His death, Jesus had promised the apostles that He would send the Helper, the promised Holy Spirit who would be with them forever (John 14:16). The Holy Spirit would help them remember the things that Jesus had said (John 14:26) and equip the apostles to record these things in the Bible and teach them to others. Jesus also said that the Helper would not come until He went away. Only after Jesus was gone, would the Helper begin His work of convicting the world of sin, revealing righteousness and judgment (John 16:7–11).

Jesus was now gone and the disciples were waiting to receive the promised Spirit. It was the day of Pentecost. The English word "Pentecost" is a transliteration of the Greek word pentekostos, which means "fifty." The word Pentecost was used by Greek-speaking Jews to refer to a Jewish holiday known as the Festival of Weeks, or, more simply, Weeks (Shavuot in Hebrew). This name comes from an expression in Leviticus 23:16, which instructs people to count seven weeks or "fifty days" from the end of Passover to the beginning of the next holiday.

Shavuot, (Pentecost) the second great feast in Israel's yearly cycle of holy days, was originally a harvest festival (Exodus 23:16), but, in time, turned into a day to commemorate the giving of the Law on Mt. Sinai. This was a major holiday for the Jews. Men from many nations were in Jerusalem as all males were required to travel to the sanctuary to worship on this holiday.

The disciples were gathered in one place for their observance of this first Pentecost since Jesus had died. They suddenly heard a sound from heaven, it was like rushing wind, and it filled the house. This rushing wind was accompanied by what appeared to be tongues of fire that came to rest above each of the disciples' heads. As they marveled at these things, they were filled with the promised Holy Spirit. And then they began to speak with other tongues. Now because this was the major holiday of the Pentecost, there were devout men there from many different nations. They heard the apostles speaking and were confused at what they heard because everyone heard them speak in their own language. It was an amazing and marvelous thing as they realized Jesus's apostles, the Galileans, were speaking, and yet all of the men heard them in their own language (Acts 2:1–8).

The Holy Spirit had come to Jesus's disciples, just as Jesus promised He would. And the Bible teaches that everyone who trusts in Jesus Christ through the word of truth, the gospel of God's salvation, will be sealed with the same Holy Spirit Jesus promised to His apostles. The Holy Spirit is a guarantee to believers of the promised inheritance—that is, the glory of eternity with God in heaven (Ephesians 1:13–14). Every believer in Jesus Christ has the Holy Spirit living in him (John 14:17).

The Holy Spirit not only lives with the believer but He works in a believer's life. He does this by changing the character, the wants, and the desires of the one who was saved—He enables the believer to become the new creation in Christ promised in 2 Corinthians 5:17. And every true believer, being a new creation in Christ and indwelt by the Holy Spirit, will manifest the good fruit of the Spirit. This fruit includes love, joy, peace, longsuffering, kindness, goodness, faithfulness, gentleness, and self-control (Galatians 5:22–23).

We must keep in mind that the Bible tells us this is the Spirit's fruit. It is brought forth in our lives ONLY for those who trust in Jesus. We could not bear more of the Spirit's fruit (or any fruit) to God's glory without the presence of the Holy Spirit in our lives. In fact, this fruit is directed by God the Father. And in order to allow it to grow in our lives, we must abide in the true vine, Jesus Christ. For without Him we would bear no fruit at all (John 15:-15–6).

HISTORICAL/APOLOGETICS BACKGROUND

To understand the significance of Acts 2 and the first Pentecost, we need to look at the final words of Jesus before He ascended to heaven in Acts 1:4–5:

And being assembled together with them, He commanded them not to depart from Jerusalem, but to wait for the Promise of the Father, "which," He said, "you have heard from Me; for John truly baptized with water, but you shall be baptized with the Holy Spirit not many days from now."

Jesus promised that the power of the Holy Spirit would come upon them. They would be given the boldness to go out and be witnesses for Jesus in Jerusalem, and in all Judea and Samaria, and to the end of the earth. After He had spoken these things, He ascended to His Father (Acts 1:8–9).

The future ministry of the disciples depended on them receiving the Holy Spirit and relying on His power. Jesus promised that the Holy Spirit of truth, the Helper, would abide with them forever. This Spirit, who had dwelt WITH them, would now be IN them (John 14:16–17).

In the same way, all believers, at the moment of salvation, are baptized in the Spirit. When we believe, we are sealed with the Holy Spirit of promise (Ephesians 1:13–14). This baptism of the Spirit is a one-time event. Paul told the Corinthians, "For by one Spirit we were all baptized into one body, whether Jews or Greeks, whether slaves or free, and we were all made to drink of one Spirit" (1 Corinthians 12:13). The New Testament does not command believers to be baptized with the Holy Spirit. It is not an experience we are to seek, but rather it is God's action performed on the believer at the moment of regeneration. Believers are, however, commanded to be filled with the Spirit, which means to be controlled by the Spirit (Ephesians 5:18). To be filled with the Spirit involves confessing all known sin and dying to self. We yield ourselves fully to the Lord and depend on Him step by step as we walk in the Spirit (Galatians 5:16). As we walk in the Spirit we will manifest the fruit of the Spirit—love, joy, peace, longsuffering, kindness, goodness, faithfulness, gentleness, and self-control (Galatians 5:22–23). This fruit will in turn show itself clearly as we live a life pleasing to God (Colossians 1:10), conformed to the image of Christ (Romans 8:29), and in right relationship with those around us (Colossians 3:16–4:1).

It is staggering to see God's providence at work throughout the Bible. And Pentecost is no different. God had providentially ordained that it would be during Pentecost that the Holy Spirit would descend from heaven. And during this time there were men from many countries present. Acts 2 mentions Mesopotamia, Judea, Cappadocia, Pontus, Asia, Phrygia, Pamphylia, Egypt, Libya, and Rome. This list of nations recorded in Acts reminds us of the list of nations in Genesis 10 at the Tower of Babel judgment. At Babel, God confused the language and dispersed the people around the world as judgment for their foolish pride. Now, at Pentecost, by His grace, God reversed the confusion experienced at Babel with the miracle of speaking in tongues. Now people of all languages could understand! And God's purpose that the gospel be spread to all nations was launched way beyond the borders of Jerusalem to many nations as the men in Jerusalem that day returned to their homes.

In fact, the Bible tells us that Peter preached the gospel, and 3,000 souls were baptized and added to the church (Acts 2:40–41). It must have been a glorious time as the apostles saw the fruit of their labors so quickly and so abundantly—all by the power of the Holy Spirit.

However, not all men responded positively to Peter's preaching that day, in spite of the miracle of the languages. Even miracles will not convince mockers, who do not want to submit their lives to the lordship of Christ. And throughout the Book of Acts, we read of powerful conversions, but also violent opposition to the preaching of the gospel. As Christians we can expect the same response. But our confidence must remain in the sovereign, holy God and in the message of Jesus Christ whose name will demand that every knee will bow before Him, and every tongue will confess Him as Lord to the glory of God the Father (Philippians 2:9–11).

For more information on this topic, see the Online Resource Page.

 Studying God's Word

Why did Jesus send the Holy Spirit?

_____

_____

Take notes as you study the following passages.

John 16:5–15

_____

_____

_____

Acts 1:3–8

_____

_____

_____

Acts 2:1–24

_____

_____

_____

 The Work of the Spirit

For each of the following passages, make a note of the role of the Holy Spirit in the life of believers.

1. Ephesians 1:13–14

2.   Galatians 5:22–26

3.   John 14:15–18

4.   1 Corinthians 2:10–16

5.   1 Corinthians 12:4–11

6.   Romans 8:12–17

Other passages to consider: 1 Corinthians 12; Acts 7:51, 13:2–4, 15:28, 20:28; 2 Timothy 1:14; John 3:5–8, 14:26; Ephesians 3:16, 4:3–4, 4:30, 5:18; Romans 8:9–11, 8:26–27, 15:16

Take notes as you study the following passage.

Matthew 23:1–36

_____

_____

_____

_____

_____

 # God's Word in the Real World

1. As you consider the work of the Holy Spirit, how has your thinking changed from the time that you were first saved (or even before your salvation)?

2. How has your understanding of the work of the Spirit changed as a result of what we have discussed today?

3. How are the events at Pentecost a reversal of the events of Babel?

4. Peter stood before the crowd in Jerusalem and immediately jumped to an Old Testament prophet to explain the events they were seeing. Would the same type of proclamation be understood if we stood up on a bench in a park in our city?

5. Peter preached in power before the crowd, boldly proclaiming truth rather than denying Christ. What changed between the night of Jesus's arrest, when Peter denied knowing Christ, and his preaching at Pentecost?

6. As you consider your own life and the fact that if you are in Christ then the Spirit of God is living in you, how are your own thoughts and actions out of sync with that truth? What can you do to change your thoughts and actions in this area?

7. Gandhi is often held up as a wonderful example of a peaceful man. Was he demonstrating the Spirit's fruit of peace? Why or why not? Should Christians be seeking to emulate Gandhi?

Prayer Requests

The Apostles Are Persecuted

9

Key Passages

- Acts 4:1–31, 6:8–15, 7:51–60

What You Will Learn

- Why the apostles were persecuted.
- How the apostles responded to persecution.

Lesson Overview

Soon after Pentecost, the apostles began to experience persecution because they preached the truth in the name of Jesus Christ. They were able to stand firm and even rejoice in their sufferings because they were empowered with the promised Holy Spirit.

Memory Verse

Romans 1:16–17

For I am not ashamed of the gospel of Christ, for it is the power of God to salvation for everyone who believes, for the Jew first and also for the Greek. For in it the righteousness of God is revealed from faith to faith; as it is written, "The just shall live by faith."

Prepare to Learn

SCRIPTURAL BACKGROUND

Jesus promised that the Holy Spirit would come to teach all things. But He would not come until Jesus had left the earth (John 16:7). And when He did come, He would guide believers into all truth (John 16:13). The Holy Spirit would empower the disciples and make them witnesses for Jesus and the gospel from Jerusalem, in all Judea and Samaria, and to the end of the earth (Acts 1:8).

As the church began to grow, so did the opposition to the truth about Jesus. The disciples drew on the power of the Holy Spirit for wisdom, strength, and perseverance as they stood firm to proclaim the faith that was once for all delivered to the saints (1 Corinthians 2:13; Ephesians 3:16; Jude 3).

It appeared the apostles were off to a good start by the power of the Holy Spirit. Peter's sermon at Pentecost added about 3,000 souls to the church (Acts 2:41). And the Bible tells us that Peter and John were given the power to heal a lame man at the Temple in the name of Jesus Christ. This lame man got up, and all the people saw him walking and praising God (Acts 3:1–10). The people were amazed at the miracle performed by the apostles, but Peter quickly declared that it was by faith in the name of Jesus Christ—the very Man they had denied and killed—that the lame man had been healed (Acts 3:15–16).

As their fame grew and they continued to preach the power of Jesus Christ and His resurrection from the dead, the priests and Jewish leaders became jealous. It wasn't long before Peter and John were arrested—but not before 5,000 more believers were added to the church (Acts 4:1–4).

A familiar scene—reminiscent of Jesus's own recent illegal trial—followed their arrest as the rulers, elders, scribes, Annas the high priest, Caiaphas, and others gathered together to question the apostles. They asked, "By what power or by what name have you done this?" (Acts 4:5–7).

God's Word tells us that Peter, filled with the wisdom and knowledge of the Holy Spirit, stood and again proclaimed that it was by the name of Jesus Christ of Nazareth, whom they had crucified and God had raised from the dead, that the man had been healed. Peter spoke boldly to his accusers in the name of Jesus, and proclaimed that salvation could be found in NO other name given to men under heaven (Acts 4:8–12).

The Jewish council was perplexed. A notable miracle had been done, and no one could deny it. But they plotted to stop the spread of this gospel of Jesus Christ, and they threatened the apostles, commanding them not to speak or teach in the name of Jesus! However, Peter and John would NOT be discouraged. And they would not back down from speaking the things they had seen and heard (Acts 4:20).

The apostles were released and went back to their friends, and together they rejoiced at God's faithfulness. As they were gathered together, they prayed that the Lord would grant them boldness to speak His Word and continue to give them the power to do signs and wonders in the name of the Lord Jesus Christ (Acts 4:23–30).

This would not be the end of their troubles, however. They were again imprisoned but miraculously freed by an angel of the Lord who opened the prison doors. The apostles went back to the Temple and began preaching again (Acts 5:17–21). Again they were arrested and told to STOP peaching in the name of Jesus Christ! And yet, the apostles boldly proclaimed that they were to obey God rather than men and would not stop preaching (Acts 5:29).

The persecution of the church and the apostles would only continue to grow worse. But even in spite of beatings and imprisonment, the apostles rejoiced that they were counted worthy to suffer shame for the name of Jesus (Acts 5:40–41).

Later on, the Apostle Paul also suffered many trials as he was persecuted for his faith in Jesus Christ. It was Paul who penned what has come to be a cry of confidence and victory in the gospel. We read it in Romans 1:16: "For I am not ashamed of the gospel of Christ, for it is the power of God to salvation for everyone who believes, for the Jew first and also for the Greek."

As Christians, we too should boldly proclaim that we will not be ashamed of the gospel of Jesus Christ. For it was through its truth that we were saved and through its power that others will be saved to eternal life.

HISTORICAL/APOLOGETICS BACKGROUND

In our Western world, Christians know very little of persecution. As Americans, we enjoy religious freedom, freedom of assembly, and freedom of speech. There are more than 450,000 churches across the United States where we can worship without government interference. Some of these are mega-churches with coffee bars, fitness centers, bookstores, and more. When we complain of being persecuted, it may be because someone called us a name, or we were denied a promotion at our job due to our evangelistic fervor.

But compared to the early church, and much of the church today around the world, we live in very peaceful and accommodating circumstances.

The history of the church is one of persecution and martyrdom. It has been customary for church historians to count ten major periods of severe persecution in the early church, beginning with the persecution under Emperor Nero in AD 64 and ending with Emperor Diocletian in AD 305. Christians were thrown to the lions, forced into gladiatorial battles, burned alive, and crucified. In fact, all of the original apostles, except John, died unnatural deaths because of their faith. And John died while exiled to the island of Patmos. In the second century, one Christian apologist wrote the following:

> Though beheaded, and crucified, and thrown to wild beasts, and chains, and fire, and all other kinds of torture, we do not give up our confession; but, the more such things happen, the more do others in larger numbers become faithful (Justin Martyr, Dialogue with Trypho).

Indeed, the history of the church demonstrates triumph in the face of persecution and martyrdom. In many places around the world, as the persecution increased, the church grew. Under Chairman Mao and Chinese Communism, for example, professing Christians in China grew from 1.5 million in 1970 to 65 million in just twenty years, even though foreign missionaries were severely restricted.

When we survey the Bible, we quickly see that persecution is a stark reality of the Christian life. The Apostle Paul warned Timothy that "everyone who wants to live a godly life in Christ Jesus will be persecuted" (2 Timothy 3:12). Jesus told His disciples to expect persecution from the world because, since they hated Him, they will hate His followers also. He said that if they persecuted Him, they would persecute His followers (John 15:18–20). Since the world is driven by the love of sin and self, it is no wonder they hate Christians who are called to be different and separate from the world. It is this very separation from the world and the world system that provokes hatred toward us.

As Christians, we must learn to recognize the spiritual value persecution offers and even to rejoice in it. Persecution allows us to share in a unique fellowship with our Lord. Paul, in his letter to the Philippians, listed a number of things he surrendered for the cause of Christ. Such losses, however, he viewed as "rubbish" (Philippians 3:8) that he might share in the "fellowship of [Christ's] sufferings" (Philippians 3:10). Peter wrote that the church should not think it strange to come upon trials, but they should rejoice that they can partake in Christ's sufferings. And, when the time comes for His glory to be revealed, those who suffered for His sake may also be glad with exceeding joy (1 Peter 4:13).

Persecution is good for our spiritual growth, whether we like to think of it that way or not. James instructs us to count it all joy when we fall into trials, knowing that the testing of our faith produces patience, endurance, and maturity (James 1:2–4). Jesus also addressed this topic during His famous Sermon on the Mount when He said that His followers would be blessed when people insult and persecute them. In fact, He said we should rejoice at persecution, for our reward will be great in heaven (Matthew 5:11–12).

It is hard to say just when we will fall into life threatening trials for the sake of the gospel. But, when it happens, we can be confident that if we are truly saved and indwelt by the Holy Spirit, His power in us will enable us to stand firm for our faith.

For more information on this topic, see the Online Resource Page.

Studying God's Word

How should Christians respond to persecution?

_____

_____

Take notes as you study the following passages.

Acts 4:1–31

_____

_____

_____

_____

Luke 21:12–18

_____

_____

_____

_____

Facing Persecution

"All who desire to live godly in Christ Jesus will suffer persecution" (2 Timothy 3:12).

If we stop to think about that verse, it might cause us to examine our hearts and ask if we are really living a life of godliness. Read the verses below from your Bible, and then answer the questions that follow based on what you read.

1 Peter 3:14–17, 4:12–16; John 15:18–25

1. How are you facing persecution for your faith in Jesus?

2. If you are not currently facing persecution, does that necessarily mean that you are not living a life of godliness? Explain your thinking.

3. What is the difference between being persecuted for our beliefs and expressions of our faith before others and being persecuted for our attitude before others?

4. How do your own attitudes about persecution compare to what is expressed in these passages?

5. If persecution comes, do you believe you will be prepared to respond to it in a way that honors Christ?

Take notes as you study the following passage.

Acts 6:8–15, 7:51–60

_____

_____

_____

_____

 God's Word in the Real World

1. How has your understanding of persecution changed as a result of looking at these passages?

2. Are there times in your life when you have hidden your faith or failed to speak up because you were afraid of what might happen as a result? How should you respond to such failures?

3. When we think about the Apostle Paul, we might think of him as a bold man who proclaimed and lived for Christ in the face of extreme threats. But, in his epistles, Paul asked the churches to pray for boldness for him as he proclaimed the gospel (Colossians 4:2–6; Ephesians 6:18–20; Philippians 1:12–26). How can we use this to encourage us to live godly lives and prepare for the persecution that may come as a result?

4. In what ways can we work together as a body to encourage one another as we face various persecutions?

5. Should we be praying that persecution DOES NOT come to us, or that we would have the grace of God we need WHEN it comes to us?

6. In what ways can we stay connected to the persecution of Christians that is happening around the world, seeking to support those who are facing immediate persecution?

Prayer Requests

_____

_____

_____

_____

_____

_____

_____

_____

_____

10
The Gospel Spreads

Key Passages

- Acts 8:1–8, 8:26–40; Romans 8:28–30

What You Will Learn

- How the gospel spread in Samaria.
- How the gospel spread to Ethiopia.

Lesson Overview

The followers of Jesus were being persecuted in Jerusalem for their faith and belief in Jesus Christ. However, God used it for good. The Christians were scattered as they left their homes to avoid the persecution. And as they moved, the gospel moved with them and spread quickly. In addition to this, God used Philip in a special way. Philip preached to the Ethiopian official who believed, was baptized, and likely took the gospel back to Ethiopia!

Memory Verse

Romans 1:16–17

For I am not ashamed of the gospel of Christ, for it is the power of God to salvation for everyone who believes, for the Jew first and also for the Greek. For in it the righteousness of God is revealed from faith to faith; as it is written, "The just shall live by faith."

Prepare to Learn

SCRIPTURAL BACKGROUND

Just before His ascension back to heaven, Jesus gave His disciples one last command. They were to go and make disciples of all nations, teaching others to observe the things Jesus had commanded. In light of this command, Jesus promised He would be with them always (Matthew 28:18–20). Not only that, but Jesus had promised the Holy Spirit would come and help them to carry out this last command (John 16:7–8; Acts 1:8). And on the day of Pentecost, in Jerusalem, the apostles were filled with the Holy Spirit, began to preach, and many were added to the church (Acts 2:41).

Things quickly changed in Jerusalem. The atmosphere for Jesus's followers was rapidly becoming quite tense. The disciples were gaining popularity, and the Lord was adding to the church daily by bringing believers to repentance and faith in Jesus Christ (Acts 2:47). This was unacceptable in the eyes of the priests, the captain of the Temple, and the Sadducees. These men were disturbed that the truth about Jesus Christ—His life, death, and Resurrection—was being preached and being believed. And they made it their mission to stop the apostles from preaching (Acts 4:2–3). The disciples were arrested and forbidden to preach in the name of Jesus Christ (Acts 4:17–18). But, the arrests, criticism, and condemnation only served to make the apostles more bold in their preaching as they prayed for the help and courage the Holy Spirit could bring (Acts 4:29–31).

As the apostles continued to preach, the religious leaders became even angrier. The tensions continued to rise until Stephen, the first martyr for Jesus,

was dragged from the city and stoned to death for proclaiming the gospel (Acts 7:54–59). Things went from bad to worse for the Christians, and they were scattered throughout the regions of Judea and Samaria because of the violent persecution (Acts 8:1–3).

So what was going on? What was God's plan? Why were Jesus's followers being arrested, beaten, killed, and run out of town? The answer? So the Word and truth about Jesus Christ would spread—and spread quickly. Until now not many had preached Jesus in Judea and Samaria. But here we read that those who were scattered went everywhere preaching the Word. The Bible tells us specifically about Philip who went down to the city of Samaria, where he was able to preach Christ, minister to the people, and bring joy in the truth to that city (Acts 8:4–8).

The Bible also tells us of God's supernatural intervention, through the appearance of an angel, to send Philip on another missionary trip to the south along the road from Jerusalem to Gaza. As he journeyed, Philip was given the opportunity to preach to an Ethiopian eunuch. This man of Ethiopia listened to Philip as he explained the book of Isaiah and clarified that it was Jesus Christ of whom the prophet Isaiah was writing. The Ethiopian believed what he heard about Jesus and was baptized, right there and then! And because he was a man of great authority in Ethiopia who worked for Queen Candace, it is likely his testimony and changed life did much to further the gospel in that region (Acts 8:27).

The early Christians were suffering severe persecution—even to death. They ran for their lives from their persecutors. But God was working. What the believers were experiencing would actually further the spread of the gospel and grow the church, not only into Judea and Samaria, as mentioned in Acts 8:1, but also beyond to the Gentiles, as we see in Acts 11:19–21:

> Now those who were scattered after the persecution that arose over Stephen traveled as far as Phoenicia, Cyprus, and Antioch, preaching the word to no one but the Jews only. But some of them were men from Cyprus and Cyrene, who, when they had come to Antioch, spoke to the Hellenists [Gentiles], preaching the Lord Jesus. And the hand of the Lord was with them, and a great number believed and turned to the Lord.

Persecution is real. And in God's goodness and sovereignty, He ordains persecution and uses it to grow His church and fulfill the Great Commission. It started in the first century, when the Christians were scattered and went everywhere preaching the word (Acts 8:1). And it continues today.

HISTORICAL/APOLOGETICS BACKGROUND

God is committed to His purposes, one of which is to reach all nations with the good news of the life, death, and Resurrection of His Son, Jesus Christ. Though God never directly persecutes His people, He does allow persecution to serve His own good purposes.

In the early chapters of Acts, we see how the Jerusalem church enjoyed wonderful fellowship and had a good reputation. There was strong unity among believers. Through the church there was powerful preaching of the kingdom of God (Acts 2:46–47). The Bible tells us that mighty, miraculous signs and wonders were being done by the apostles. People were being healed, the Word was spreading, and multitudes of men and women were being added to the church (Acts 5:12–16). Who would want to leave a church like that? These church members in Jerusalem, no doubt, were basking in the blessings of God.

But Jesus had promised the coming of the Holy Spirit who would empower His people to be His witnesses not only in Jerusalem but also to Judea, Samaria, and far beyond its borders (Acts 1:8). And He had commissioned His disciples to go and make disciples of the nations (Matthew 28:19–20).

So, what did God do? He used the persecution of these early believers to get them to leave the comfort of their homes and the blessing of a thriving fellowship as they sought to avoid imprisonment, torture, and often death. As they fled, their faith was strengthened, and the truth of Jesus Christ went with them as they journeyed to distant lands. In this, God's plan to preach the gospel to all nations was being carried out. The church may well have eventually awakened to her calling to send missionaries to other lands, but for now, God would use this season of persecution to motivate His people to grow His church.

God's will was done! And the Christians who were scattered because of the persecution went everywhere preaching the Word (Acts 8:4).

The truth spread first into Judea and Samaria and, by the third century, had extended into what we know today as Western Europe, North Africa, Eastern Europe, Southwest Asia, Central Asia, and India.

Church history tells us of the journeys of apostles and other church leaders as they endeavored to fulfill Jesus's Great Commission. There is some tradition that James, the brother of John, may have traveled to Spain and established churches there before returning to Jerusalem. Thomas is said to have traveled to India with the gospel. In fact, the churches of western India trace their origins to Thomas and refer to themselves as the Thomas Church. Tradition also puts Bartholomew in India where he was eventually martyred. Thaddeus is said to have ministered in Armenia. And others traveled far and wide with the life-giving gospel—all prompted by the persecution experienced in the first century.

Whenever persecution has come, and God's people have been scattered, the gospel has gone with them. In fact, it has been said that ease and comfort are enemies of the gospel more than need and persecution. We are witnessing that in our culture today as churches focus more on how large they can become and what innovative technology they can use to attract the culture, seeming to care less about taking the saving message of the true gospel to those who need so desperately to hear it.

Often comfort, ease, affluence, and prosperity cause terrible apathy in the church. Material blessings that should produce more personnel, more energy, and more funds for the cause of Christ and His kingdom often produce the exact opposite—weakness, indifference, laziness, self-centeredness, and preoccupation with security.

The Bible has much to say about loving the world (1 John 2:15) and building up for ourselves treasures on earth (Matthew 6:19). We are warned by the Apostle Paul in 1 Timothy 6:10 that, "the love of money is a root of all kinds of evil." Interestingly, recent studies have shown that it is low-income families that are the most generous group in America. The poorest fifth of U.S. households contribute an average of 4.3 percent of their incomes to charitable organizations. The richest fifth give just 2.1 percent. In other words, the poorest members of the church are twice as generous as the richest members. Some might say we are too comfortable and too wealthy to understand the urgency of the gospel.

What is the answer? It would not be to seek persecution, for God alone knows when each of us is ready to stand up under the evils of the wicked one (Ephesians 6:13). But we can examine our own hearts and ask ourselves some penetrating questions: Is the prosperity of our culture and our churches furthering the cause of Christ, or is it a hindrance to self-sacrifice in taking the gospel to other lands? How does our personal giving to missions and to the church compare to the rest of our spending? Does it reflect Christ's command to preach the gospel to all nations? And, are we prepared to suffer for Christ in order to grow His church?

For more information on this topic, see the Online Resource Page.

Studying God's Word

How does persecution promote the spread of the gospel?

_____

Take notes as you study the following passages.

Acts 8:1–8

_____

_____

_____

_____

1 Peter 1:1–2

_____

_____

_____

Acts 8:26–40

_____

_____

_____

_____

Romans 10:14–17

_____

_____

_____

_____

# Providential Outcomes

As we see in the book of Acts, God providentially directs the events of man in a way that brings about His purposes on the earth. Sometimes those events are desirable, but God also uses what the Puritans called "bitter providences" to work His plans in the world. While we often think of Romans 8:28–30 as a verse that talks of overcoming personal trials, there is a much broader application to consider. Read the verses below in light of the persecution that faced the Jerusalem Christians and answer the following questions.

1. When you consider the persecution of the early church in Jerusalem, how do the principles of Romans 8:28–30 apply to what was happening?

2. How does this principle relate to Joseph's words in Genesis 50:20?

3. How does the persecution connect to the words of Jesus in John 10:16?

4. As you consider all the circumstances and all the people involved in the different aspects of the spreading of the gospel in the early part of Acts, how does this help you to understand the sovereignty and wisdom of God?

Take notes as you study the following passage.

John 18:1–9

_____

_____

_____

_____

 # God's Word in the Real World

1. Think about our world today. Where do you see the gospel spreading as the result of persecution or simply by faithful witnesses proclaiming it to others?

2. Many people today believe that the gospel cannot be preached unless you first build friendships with people. How do these accounts of Philip show that idea to be false?

3. How have you seen God at work in you to spread the gospel?

4. How do you identify with Philip? Are you ready and willing to go where the gospel needs to be proclaimed?

5. As you understand more about how God has providentially worked in history, how should you respond to that understanding?

Prayer Requests

11
Saul Is Converted

Key Passages

- Acts 8:1–3, 9:1–33; 1 Timothy 1:13;
  1 Corinthians 15:9; 2 Corinthians 5:17;
  Galatians 1:10–17

What You Will Learn

- How Saul was converted.

- What Saul/Paul was like before and after his conversion.

Lesson Overview

Jesus appeared to Saul in a bright light. When confronted with the truth of who Jesus is, Saul became a believer. His life changed from a persecutor to a preacher of the gospel of Jesus Christ, and he endured many trials for preaching truth by the grace of God.

Memory Verse

Romans 1:16–17

For I am not ashamed of the gospel of Christ, for it is the power of God to salvation for everyone who believes, for the Jew first and also for the Greek. For in it the righteousness of God is revealed from faith to faith; as it is written, "The just shall live by faith."

Prepare to Learn

SCRIPTURAL BACKGROUND

All believers who heed the words of Jesus Christ to repent and believe in the gospel (Mark 1:15) become new creations in Christ Jesus—the old is gone and the new has come (2 Corinthians 5:17). Believers are born again to a living hope through the Resurrection of Jesus Christ from the dead (1 Peter 1:3). How this happens in the hearts of each individual is a work of God. Each transformation is dramatic in that God seals the soul of the believer for eternity (Ephesians 1:13–14).

However, some circumstances that surround the conversion of each believer may not seem as dramatic as others. God redeems some at a very young age from a Christian family, others attend church all their lives, they live lives honoring to God, and then one day they understand the truth of the gospel as they repent and turn to Christ as Savior. Still others live lives of darkness, sin, and rebellion—and God reveals His truth to them suddenly and unexpectedly bringing them out of the darkness and into the light (John 8:12).

But there have been few conversion experiences that would top that of the Jew, Saul of Tarsus, who boasted of his confidence in his life and background. He had been circumcised according to Jewish law. He was a Hebrew of Hebrews, a descendant of Benjamin, of the house of Abraham—a true son of Israel. As a Pharisee, he was zealous for the Jewish law and openly and passionately persecuted the church—those who proclaimed Jesus as Lord (Philippians 3:4–6).

And yet, he was dramatically transformed into a new creation in Christ and then used by God to start numerous churches and write much of the New Testament. How did the Lord Jesus Christ get this murderous Pharisee's attention? It happened on the road to Damascus where Saul fully intended to find men and women of the Way (followers of Jesus) and bring them bound to Jerusalem for persecution and trial (Acts 9:1–2).

Jesus literally knocked Saul to the ground as he journeyed. He saw a bright light and heard a voice speaking to him, the Lord Jesus Himself, asking, "Saul, Saul, why are your persecuting Me?" (Acts 9:3–4). Saul was astonished and afraid—to the point of asking what the Lord would have him do. The Lord had something for him—and it would start in the city of Damascus, the very city he was headed to in order to further destroy the church and the people of Christ. But the Lord's plan was far different than Saul's plan. Saul had been struck down and humbled and was afraid. The Lord had made him blind, and Saul was helplessly led by the hand into the city (Acts 9:8).

The zealous Pharisee, Saul, had met the risen Christ who called him into ministry in a spectacular way. The Lord declared that Saul (whose name was changed to Paul following his conversion) was His chosen vessel, and he would bear the name of Christ to the Gentiles, to kings, and to the children of Israel (Acts 9:15). Jesus had plans for Saul, and Saul's heart was dramatically changed so that, "immediately he preached Christ in the synagogues, that He [Jesus] is the Son of God" (Acts 9:20)!

Saul was a new creation in Christ. This Hebrew of Hebrews, who had persecuted the Way by binding and then delivering both men and women to prison (Acts 22:4); this Saul who had held the clothes of the murderers as they dragged the very first martyr for Christ, Stephen, out of the city and stoned him because of his faith and love for Jesus (Acts 7:57–59); this man now suffered for His Lord through beatings, stonings, shipwrecks, peril, robbers, weariness, toil, sleeplessness, hunger, thirst, cold, nakedness, and many other things (2 Corinthians 11:25–27). The Lord Jesus Christ had made Paul a new creation. And after meeting the living Jesus, he would no longer boast except in the Cross of the Lord Jesus Christ (Galatians 6:14).

HISTORICAL/APOLOGETICS BACKGROUND

If anyone deserves to be punished and to pay for his sins, it would be a person who has persecuted believers, hunted them down, imprisoned them, assisted with their murder, and blasphemed the name of God. Right? That may be how we think sometimes, but the truth is that all of us have sinned and fall short of the glory of God (Romans 3:23). All sin is an affront to a holy God, no matter how small we think it may be, or how vile. The fact is, God's grace is greater than all our sin— than any sin. No sin is too vile that God cannot forgive it, and no sinner is so bad that God cannot redeem him.

We see this played out in the life of Saul of Tarsus. Saul was a fervently religious Jew who thought he was serving God by persecuting members of a new sect. They called themselves The Way (Acts 9:2, 19:9), and they claimed that their leader, who had been crucified for claiming to be God, had risen from the dead. Further, they were preaching that only by faith in this Man's name— Jesus—could anyone be saved. Saul would not believe the Man's "lies" and was zealously persecuting the followers of Jesus, even to the point of entering houses and dragging off men and women to prison (Acts 8:3).

It was in the context of Saul's ongoing, zealous persecution of the church that he encountered the risen Christ on the road to Damascus (Acts 9). After his vision of Jesus and sudden conversion, the blinded Saul was told to go into the city of Damascus and to wait for instructions. Several days later, Jesus appeared to a disciple named Ananias and told him to go lay his hands on Saul so that he would receive his sight. Ananias responded as we might respond. He said something like, "What? You mean the Saul of Tarsus who has been persecuting the church and killing the saints?! You mean the guy who came here with the purpose of imprisoning believers?!" And Jesus replied to him, "Go, for he is a chosen vessel of Mine to bear My name before Gentiles, kings, and the children of Israel. For I will show him how many things he must suffer for My name's sake" (Acts 9:15–16).

Years later, while writing to his young disciple Timothy, Saul, now renamed Paul, would recount his conversion experience:

> And I thank Christ Jesus our Lord who has enabled me, because He counted me faithful, putting me into the ministry, although I was formerly a blasphemer, a persecutor, and an insolent man; but I obtained mercy because I did it ignorantly in unbelief. And the grace of our Lord was exceedingly abundant, with faith and love which are in Christ Jesus. This is a faithful saying and worthy of all acceptance, that Christ Jesus came into the world to save sinners, of whom I am chief. However, for this reason I obtained mercy, that in me first Jesus Christ

might show all longsuffering, as a pattern to those who are going to believe on Him for everlasting life (1 Timothy 1:12–16).

The grace of the Lord Jesus Christ is "exceedingly abundant" toward sinners—all sinners. That was the reason Jesus came to earth, lived a perfect life, and then suffered and died—to save sinners. There is no sin too great that God cannot forgive, and no sinner so bad that God cannot change. God delights in taking persecutors and turning them into worshippers.

Paul said that he had obtained mercy that he might be an example of the great patience of Christ for those who would believe. And He serves as an example for all of us who do believe. If we think that God will not forgive us, or someone we know and love, for some sin, we can think of Paul. And remember that Jesus is all-forgiving; His death on the Cross is sufficient payment for ALL the sins of those who repent and turn to Him.

All sinners will be judged. As Paul told the Corinthians:

Do you not know that the unrighteous will not inherit the kingdom of God? Do not be deceived. Neither fornicators, nor idolaters, nor adulterers, nor homosexuals, nor sodomites, nor thieves, nor covetous, nor drunkards, nor revilers, nor extortioners will inherit the kingdom of God (1 Corinthians 6:9–10).

But, we can thank God that those who have repented of their sins and trusted in Christ—in His perfect life, His substitutionary death, and His powerful Resurrection—are forgiven, washed, cleansed, and made righteous because of what Jesus did on the Cross. Paul followed this bad news of judgment to the Corinthians with the good news of forgiveness.

And such were some of you. But you were washed, but you were sanctified, but you were justified in the name of the Lord Jesus and by the Spirit of our God (1 Corinthians 6:11).

There is no sin we might commit that is so great that it is beyond the reach of God's forgiveness in Jesus Christ. And there is no person who is so wicked that the grace of God may not touch His heart to convert him. No! Jesus is exceedingly abundant in grace. He died that men could be forgiven. As the writer of this hymn so elegantly wrote:

Marvelous grace of our loving Lord,

Grace that exceeds our sin and our guilt!

Yonder on Calvary's mount outpoured,

There where the blood of the Lamb was spilt.

Grace, grace, God's grace,

Grace that will pardon and cleanse within;

Grace, grace, God's grace,

Grace that is greater than all our sin!

For more information on this topic, see the Online Resource Page.

# Studying God's Word

Is one person's salvation more miraculous than another's?

_____

Take notes as you study the following passages.

Acts 9:1–9

_____

_____

_____

_____

_____

Acts 26:9–18

_____

_____

_____

_____

_____

Acts 9:10–30

_____

_____

_____

_____

_____

 Testimony of Mercy

Read the following passages where Paul recounts his days as the unconverted Saul and what God had done for him then answer the questions below: 1 Timothy 1:12–17; 1 Corinthians 15:9–11; Galatians 1:10–17.

1. As you read 1 Timothy 1:12–17, what stands out to you as Paul tells of his conversion?

2. What is so important about the word "but" in the middle of 1 Corinthians 15:9–11?

3. How was Paul's former life as a Jew different from his life as a Christian based on Galatians 1:10–17?

4. In all of these passages, how does Paul explain why he was called to be an apostle?

5. When you hear a testimony like Paul's or a drug dealer or prostitute being saved by Jesus, do you think your testimony is less worthy of sharing? Explain your thinking.

Take notes as you study the following passage.

Luke 14:25–33

_____

_____

_____

_____

_____

God's Word in the Real World

1. As you think about Saul's conversion, what impresses you most?

2. Some Christians speak of Jesus as a gentleman who politely knocks on the door of the unbeliever's heart asking for permission to come in. How does this idea compare to Jesus's interaction with Saul on the road to Damascus in calling him to repent and follow Him?

3. Has your attitude toward sharing your testimony changed in light of our discussion today?

4. Many people detest the idea that God would pardon a murderer or rapist and allow them to be with Him in heaven, but they think that they are good enough to get to heaven. How can you help someone who has this objection to understand what the Bible teaches about salvation?

5. In all honesty, do you struggle with the idea of God extending grace to someone like Saul? Could Hitler have been forgiven by God? Why do you deserve to be forgiven?

Prayer Requests

The Gospel Goes to the Gentiles

12

Key Passages

- Acts 10:1–48; Mark 7:14–23; 1 Timothy 4:1–5; Romans 14:1–3; Leviticus 11, 20:25–26

What You Will Learn

- The two ways people reacted to Jesus's message.

- The importance of believing in Jesus Christ as Savior and Lord.

Lesson Overview

Peter had a vision from God which taught him that salvation through Jesus Christ wasn't just for the Jews. When he was called to Cornelius's home, Peter explained the gospel to the Gentiles. All those who heard the truth believed and were baptized.

Memory Verse

Romans 1:16–17

For I am not ashamed of the gospel of Christ, for it is the power of God to salvation for everyone who believes, for the Jew first and also for the Greek. For in it the righteousness of God is revealed from faith to faith; as it is written, "The just shall live by faith."

Prepare to Learn

SCRIPTURAL BACKGROUND

The zealous Jew Saul whose name was changed to Paul was knocked down on the road to Damascus by the Lord Himself. Saul was on his way to persecute those Jews who were following the truth of the risen Jesus Christ (Acts 9:1–4). The Bible tells us that Paul was baptized, and soon after, he preached Christ in the synagogues to the other Jews.

All of the believers in the early church were Jews. Jesus was born into a Jewish family. His apostles were Jewish, and they taught, like Paul, in the synagogues to the Jewish nation.

But before Jesus left this earth, He commanded his followers to go and make disciples of all the nations (Matthew 28:19). They would receive power from the Holy Spirit as they went out to witness to all of Judea, Samaria, and to the end of the earth (Acts 1:8). This commission included the Gentiles. At this time in history, anyone not of Jewish ancestry was considered a Gentile. And the Gentiles were despised by the Jews because of their religious and cultural differences. Because of the animosity between them the only thing that could motivate the Jews to go to the Gentile nations with the good news of Christ would be the grace of God through faith.

We see this grace clearly as it plays out between the Apostle Peter and Cornelius who was a centurion in the Italian army. Their meeting was supernaturally orchestrated by God Himself as Cornelius encountered an angel of God. The angel instructed him to send messengers to Joppa to look for Peter there (Acts 10:1–5). The next day, Peter was experiencing a vision from God. In the vision Peter saw heaven open up. And a great sheet holding all kinds of four-footed animals, creeping things, and birds descended down to earth (Acts 10:11–12). Apparently, at least some of the animals Peter saw in his vision were considered "unclean" animals. This refers to animals that the Jews were not permitted to eat because of Old Testament Laws (Leviticus 20:25–26).

But Peter heard a voice (apparently the Lord) telling him to eat the animals he saw. Peter responded to the Lord saying he could not eat it. And then God spoke again, "What God has cleansed you must not call common" (Acts 10:13–14). After three "discussions" between Peter and the Lord, the object was taken up into heaven (Acts 10:16). Peter pondered the vision and what it might mean.

About this time, the men sent by Cornelius, the centurion, arrived in Joppa at the house where Peter was staying. They told Peter that he was to come to Caesarea to meet the Gentile Cornelius (Acts 10:22). Peter agreed to go. This was highly unusual as Jews would not associate with Gentiles, much less visit their homes. But Peter had learned something from his vision of the unclean food. He explains it in Acts 10:28—"Then he said to them, 'You know how unlawful it is for a Jewish man to keep company with or go to one of another nation. But God has shown me that I should not call any man common or unclean.'"

God had taught Peter an important lesson. The Lord said that what He cleansed would not be unclean, or common (Acts 10:15). And Peter acknowledged this fact when he told Cornelius that God shows no partiality between people. But whoever fears God and works righteousness is accepted by Him (Acts 10:34–35). Peter continued speaking with Cornelius about Jesus Christ—His life, His death, and His Resurrection (Acts 10:38–40).

And as Peter spoke, the Holy Spirit came upon Cornelius and the other Gentiles who were with him, and they believed in Jesus. Then Peter commanded that they be baptized in the name of the Lord. The Jews who had come with Peter were astounded that these Gentiles could come to know the truth about Jesus (Acts 10:45, 10:48).

In this amazing providential meeting, God made it clear that He accepts both Jew and Gentile into His church. And believers are, in fact, to preach to ALL nations!

HISTORICAL/APOLOGETICS BACKGROUND

Here in Acts 10, the Bible records that Peter had a vision while on a rooftop in Joppa. Peter saw something like a great sheet lowered from heaven full of unclean animals. A voice told Peter to kill and eat. His response was, "Not so, Lord! For I have never eaten anything common or unclean." Then the voice told Peter, "What God has cleansed you must not call common" (Acts 10:15). This was repeated three times. What did this strange vision mean? Even Peter wondered what the vision might mean (Acts 9:17).

To understand the meaning of the vision and Peter's response, we must go all the way back to the book of Leviticus. God, in His Law, gave His people, Israel, very strict standards regarding their diet. We read about these restrictions in Leviticus 11.

Included in the list of animals they were not to eat were the rock hyrax, the hare (the Hebrew word *arnebeth* which was an undetermined animal), and swine (Leviticus 11:5–7). The Law also forbade eating anything from the sea that didn't have fins or scales (Leviticus 11:10). There were certain flying creatures and insects they could and couldn't eat as well (Leviticus 11:13–23). As a result of these laws, Jewish thinking included a very strict division between clean and unclean animals. No self-respecting Jew, including Peter, would ever eat anything but clean animals.

Some may ask why God made a distinction between clean and unclean animals. We are not told why, but we can make some educated guesses. First, there are some animals that are more liable to carry diseases. Since the preparation of food in those days wasn't anything like it is now, God was protecting Israel from the threat of an epidemic. The Israelites lived in close community. There were millions of them, and they often traveled together. If sickness broke out, it would affect many if not the entire community.

The second reason for the dietary laws, and probably the more important one, is that God wanted to distinguish His people from the other peoples that lived around them. In those days, the primary source of entertainment was feasting, so social contact mainly occurred at large banquets. It seems that God gave the Jews these peculiar dietary laws so they wouldn't mix socially with pagan Gentiles around them. God was preventing them from having social relationships with Gentiles so that they would not adopt the pagan practices of their idolatrous neighbors.

As the restrictions on interacting with Gentiles passed away, so did the laws pertaining to restrictions on the foods that would have been involved in that interaction. In Peter's vision, God commanded him to eat of the unclean animals. While the interpretation was to see the Gentiles as "clean," there is also an immediate context of God declaring those animals clean for food. This is confirmed by Paul's recognition that all creatures of God can be received as food with thanksgiving to God (1 Timothy 4:1–5). Mark also recognized, likely in hindsight (many translations put the phrase "thus purifying all foods" as a parenthetical comment and not what Jesus spoke directly), that Jesus also taught that all foods were clean in Mark 7:19. In the New Covenant, the old dietary laws have been fulfilled for us in Christ.

In Peter's day, the Jews viewed Gentiles as unclean. A strict Jew would never be a guest in a Gentile house, nor would he invite one to his home. Even the dirt from a Gentile country was considered unclean. If anyone happened to track some Gentile dirt into Israel, it defiled the dirt of Israel. Therefore, when travelers left a Gentile country, they would always shake the dust off their feet to avoid polluting the land of Israel. That's why when Jesus sent out the seventy to preach the gospel, He told them that if anyone didn't receive their words, they were to shake the dust off their feet. In other words, they were to treat him as a Gentile (Matthew 10:5–14).

When Jesus came, He intended to make Jew and Gentile into one new man (see Ephesians 2:11–18). The deep divisions and hostility were to be a thing of the past. In Christ "there is neither Greek nor Jew, circumcised nor uncircumcised, barbarian, Scythian, slave nor free, but Christ is all and in all" (Colossians 3:11). This was an easy thing for Christ to accomplish through His life, death, and Resurrection, however, it was a very difficult thing for the Jew to practice.

God showed Peter through this vision in Acts 10 that he was no longer to divide people into categories of clean and unclean. Peter got the message and entered the house of Cornelius to share the gospel with them.

What a lesson in evangelizing and Christian living. Many Christians tend to categorize people—those who are "worthy" to hear the gospel and those who aren't; those God can save and those who are beyond help; those who are "good enough" to come to our church and those who should not be there because they are different from us. The fact is we are all sinners in need of grace. There is no one beyond the reach of God's grace and forgiveness through Jesus Christ. And we are commanded to preach the gospel and make disciples of all people, regardless of ethnicity, class, or any other distinction. This is far easier to do if we can look at people as God sees them—sinners who need to repent and turn to Christ in order to receive eternal life.

For more information on this topic, see the Online Resource Page.